Transforming Social Action into Social Change

Cohen offers a new framework for analyzing social projects and local social activism. Rather than look at how single projects are designed and managed to evaluate their impact, the approach calls for analyzing fields of social action: policy and politics, institutional behavior, social networks among policymakers and practitioners, and availability of funding and other resources. Combined, they affect the conceptualization of a social problem and the design and practice of social intervention. More broadly, through circumscribing the range of thinking about social problems, they delimit possibilities to generate social change. Analyzing fields also allows for linking macro-level trends in areas like policy to decision-making within individual organizations and the effectiveness of projects at instigating the desired transformation in individual and collective behavior.

Working together, policymakers, individual activists, nonprofit organizations, and staff in public institutions like schools and hospitals can critique and alter fields to challenge more effectively social problems. This collaboration, in turn, affects how social policies are designed and, ultimately, the politics of social change.

Shana Cohen is a Research Associate with the Department of Sociology, University of Cambridge. She holds a PhD in Sociology from the University of California, Berkeley. Cohen's research interests include the politics of social action, inequality and political identity, nonprofit management, and community development.

Transforming Social Action into Social Change
Improving Policy and Practice

Shana Cohen

Routledge
Taylor & Francis Group
NEW YORK AND LONDON

First published 2018
by Routledge
711 Third Avenue, New York, NY 10017

and by Routledge
2 Park Square, Milton Park, Abingdon, Oxon, OX14 4RN

Routledge is an imprint of the Taylor & Francis Group, an informa business

© 2018 Taylor & Francis

The right of Shana Cohen to be identified as author of this work has been asserted by her in accordance with sections 77 and 78 of the Copyright, Designs and Patents Act 1988.

All rights reserved. No part of this book may be reprinted or reproduced or utilised in any form or by any electronic, mechanical, or other means, now known or hereafter invented, including photocopying and recording, or in any information storage or retrieval system, without permission in writing from the publishers.

Trademark notice: Product or corporate names may be trademarks or registered trademarks, and are used only for identification and explanation without intent to infringe.

Library of Congress Cataloging-in-Publication Data
Names: Cohen, Shana, 1966– author.
Title: Transforming social action into social change : improving policy and practice / Shana Cohen.
Description: New York, NY : Routledge, 2017. | Includes bibliographical references.
Identifiers: LCCN 2017001668 (print) | LCCN 2017018036 (ebook) | ISBN 9781315167619 (Ebook) | ISBN 9781138050587 (hardback) | ISBN 9781138050594 (pbk.)
Subjects: LCSH: Social policy. | Social action. | Social problems. | Social change.
Classification: LCC HN18.3 (ebook) | LCC HN18.3 .C64 2017 (print) | DDC 306—dc23
LC record available at https://lccn.loc.gov/2017001668

ISBN: 978-1-138-05058-7 (hbk)
ISBN: 978-1-138-05059-4 (pbk)
ISBN: 978-1-315-16761-9 (ebk)

Typeset in Legacy Serif
by Apex CoVantage, LLC

To Rupert

CONTENTS

1 Bridging Policy and Practice — 1
2 Assessing the Context of Social Action — 48
3 Analyzing Fields of Social Action — 80
Conclusion — 119

References — 130
Index — 139

Chapter 1
BRIDGING POLICY AND PRACTICE

Several years ago, a colleague and I proposed an idea to a government ministry in the United Kingdom. We would partner with the government to create a social fund based on investment from multiple faith communities to support multi-faith social projects. The purpose of the project was to encourage cooperation between faith communities at both the funder and project delivery stages and thus promote constructive engagement in highly diverse urban areas. We proposed funding several projects within a year-long pilot stage, at perhaps a limit of £30,000 apiece, so as to develop models for interfaith work. Yet, after months of delay, the ministry decided to put the project out to tender as a replica of an existing program, which distributed small grants of a maximum of £5,000 to grassroots projects. The organization that won the bid (we decided not to apply) was a single-faith organization experimenting with more involvement in social action, in part to develop a relationship with the relevant ministry.

The trajectory of this idea, which began as a way of encouraging multi-faith engagement with social issues and ended up as a small grants program associated with one faith, reflects the challenge faced by practitioners of influencing policy and, more specifically, funding streams. Conversely, it reveals the power of policymakers and funding bodies over methods of instigating and categorizing social change. Finally, the end result suggests how nonprofit organizations and policymakers build working relationships through government funding and more informal contact. These relationships can reinforce a particular policy agenda, create a hierarchy of organizations based on their political and economic resources, and prioritize certain methods of intervention while undermining or marginalizing others.

This book analyzes social action in a number of contexts to understand how interrelated factors like policy and political ideology, institutional behavior, social networks among policymakers and practitioners, and availability of funding and other resources (such as space—for instance, churches often host winter night shelters) affect the practice of social intervention, and more broadly, possibilities to generate social change. Rather than focus on single projects, however, the book suggests that analyzing patterns across the area of work can reveal how policy and other factors influence the formation and sustainability of what I call here a 'field of social action.'

More specifically, the book proposes a conceptual framework derived from qualitative research on nonprofit (including community- and faith-based) and non-governmental organizations that links macro-level factors like policy to the expression of social values, generation and communication of knowledge, and decision-making about allocation of resources and design of activities that characterize frontline intervention in a particular area. Analyzing the correlation and contradictions between the context and the experience of project delivery within the framework of a field of social action allows for assessing how the environment affects achievement of policy aims. By investigating how practitioners perceive and act upon issues on the frontline, the framework also aims to provide the basis for developing alternative ideas, and ultimately for disrupting the circular dynamic between political elites and grassroots social action that perpetuate a field (Bruno-van Vijfeijken and Schmitz 2011; Lazar 2012).

In exploring fields of social action, the book makes several arguments. The first is that these fields are distinguishable not only because they are identified with a problem categorized and explained by policymakers and 'experts' (see O'Connor 2001; Katz 1995) like homelessness or illiteracy, but also because they are characterized by dominant methods of addressing the particular problem, such as homeless shelters and temporary housing or literacy classes. 'Field' here borrows from Bourdieu's conception (1979/1987) in that fields are sites of competition for appropriate responses to social 'problems.'[1] David Swartz defines Bourdieu's notion of fields as "arenas of production, circulation, and appropriation of goods, services, knowledge, or status, and the competitive positions held by actors in their struggle to accumulate and monopolize different kinds of capital" (1996, 79). He adds, "Field is a more inclusive concept than market; as a spatial metaphor it suggests rank and hierarchy as well as exchange relations between buyers and sellers" (1996, 79).[2] In other words, fields of social action possess their own internal dynamic, created through power relations among various actors and institutions. Similar to Bourdieu, a field of social action "contains the principle of its own transformation" (1987: 818) but not just in tension produced by the 'objective interests' of those possessing different perspectives. Transformation also occurs in the social experience of delivering a service and its contradictions with the circular dynamic of policy, funding, method of intervention, and categorization and evidence of impact reproducing of the field.

The second argument of the book is that fields of widely diverse substantive concerns—for instance, homelessness and interreligious understanding—can be analyzed using the same conceptual framework because they are generated by the same factors: policy and politics, social networks, availability of material resources, and national and local institutional behavior. These factors produce both similar organizational approaches to designing, managing, and assessing services across fields and shared methods of intervention within fields (Kamat 2004; Wright and Noble 2012; Petras 1999). This is not to dismiss the local specificities of the context or as Cadena-Roa et al. write (2011),

> We should move from thinking in terms of a general environment and start thinking in terms of specific environments or, even better, of specific fields of interaction between a given association (or sets of associations), and significant stakeholders, competitors, and institutions.
>
> (18)

The point is that the kinds of stakeholders and external actors, from schools to local governments to private foundations, remain consistent across locations.

The focus on services and how a social problem is conceptualized and addressed differs from the substantial literature that debates isomorphism among nonprofit organizations. This literature, based on an original theory by Dimaggio and Powell (1983), examines trends in similarity or diversity across organizational forms, with the current consensus that diversity prevails in the sector (see, for example, Leiter 2005). Rather than concentrate on the relationship between context and organizational form, analyzing a field of social action aims to understand the links among context, organization, the conception of a social problem, and the interventions designed to address the problem. By utilizing the concept of a field, and thus including an investigation of reproduction, the analysis explores the association between conceptions of problems and services, on the one hand, and organizational characteristics and sustainability, on the other.

Across fields, organizations utilize common methods of evaluation and categorizations of productivity and value, such as outputs (attendance or use) or outcomes (measurement of improvement or change, such as higher literacy rates). As a number of scholars have noted (Green 2014; Green and Mosse 2011; Hickey and Mohan 2004; 2005; Lewis 2014), in implementing the agenda of funding bodies, organizations adopt the discourse of concepts of intervention such as 'empowerment'[3] and incorporate training in their work that defines the orientation of staff skill development. More practically, confronted with funding body requirements, staff face pressure to limit overhead costs and concentrate collection of data on specific aspects of service delivery and use, such as completion of a program, that may not in fact account for factors critical to service effectiveness (see Chapter 2).

The ability to compare fields can be attributed to supra-national policies like the Millennium Development Goals or, their successor, the Sustainable Development Goals, which have established transnational objectives and national programs, whether launched by governments or other funders. This capacity is also due to the increase in funding bodies that have projects in multiple locations, either cities or countries; shared rules across these bodies regarding funding cycles, project design and delivery, and evaluation methods and reporting; and common training approaches that affect organizational management.

For example, United Way in the United States established a ten-year initiative in 2008 to halve the number of young people who drop out of high school.[4] This objective became part of funding priorities, targets, and generation of information in United Way's relationship with partnering local organizations. In its evaluation of one related initiative,

'Family Engagement For High School Success' (funded by AT&T), the Harvard Family Research Project (now the Global Family Research Project, and without the affiliation with Harvard)[5] mentions that it "worked closely with United Way Worldwide to chart the grantee planning process, which is divided into three parts: defining focal populations, identifying outcomes, and developing strategies to achieve these outcomes."[6] To conduct the evaluation and produce outputs like a toolkit and several reports, the project created "a milestone document to measure progress" and a "structured form to collect data from grantees as they complete each phase of the planning process."[7] The data was used to "help grantees construct clear and specific goals, strategies, and activities that are aligned with their desired outcomes." In other words, the funding body (AT&T), the organization running the program (United Way), the evaluator (Global Family Research Project), and local partners all engaged with the same forms and thus collection of data and the same circular process of linking goals to activities and then back to outcomes or achievement of goals. This dynamic underpins the formation and characteristics of a field; in this case, high school dropout prevention.

Similarly, the Moroccan national government's 2012–2015 program to combat illiteracy, particularly among rural women, has a target of reaching a million people a year and reducing the illiteracy rate to 20% by 2016. The program operates through primarily public and nonprofit providers, though the king has recently supported courses in mosques,[8] and it aims to improve training of instructors, use of appropriate methods for the location, and project evaluations as a means to achieve its goals.[9] The program itself has figured into the Millennium Development Goals (MDGs), or the eight goals set by international leaders and agencies in 2000, and thus the agendas of a number of international development agencies like the United Nations Development Program (UNDP). Like the United Way program, illiteracy projects in Morocco operate within a larger rubric established through a network of international and national actors that influence the actions of local projects through their own requirements.

The same pressures that underpin similar approaches to the management of social intervention across fields also encourage shared methods of intervention within fields. Factors like government policy or resource availability influence the design and sustainability of particular kinds of activities. For instance, night shelters during the winter in England are traditionally housed in churches.[10] They receive referrals from government or charitable agencies for what is primarily a generic activity, or one-night accommodation for transient or vulnerable populations, dependent largely on church-based volunteers and space. Other services for 'rough sleepers,' or people sleeping on the street, include day centers that provide benefits, job-seeking assistance, and other advice;[11] and some activities and showers or help lines, like that offered by Shelter, a leading homeless and housing advocacy charity in the United Kingdom.[12]

Analyzing a field entails examining diversity and commonality in intervention across projects and exploring reasons for the range of activities. As will be discussed in relation to interfaith forums, the range of projects has consequences for impact, for instance winter shelters only providing immediate relief during the cold season or advice services only providing information rather than more intensive, sustained intervention. They also reflect external constraints on innovation and thus evoke questions as to why certain interventions are not replicated or do not survive. For example, Quaker Social Action runs a support service in London that advises on how to reduce funeral costs. Its advice service differs from the few charities, like the Child Funeral Charity, which provide funds directly. Based in East London, the organization Down to Earth[13] acts as an intermediary between funeral directors, the Department of Work and Pensions—which has support funds for low-income families for bereavement and burial[14]—and the National Health Service, and families. The origin of the service itself reflects pervasive financial precariousness, the declining stigma of poverty, the expense of burial in London, and pricing by funeral chains, which tends to be too high for low-income families. Its uniqueness as a project could be attributed to lack of political interest, and thus policy initiatives, in addressing the issue, evidenced in a lack of industry regulation[15] and failure of the DWP Funeral Payments fund to match rising funeral costs.[16] Beyond political interest in the specific issue, the isolation of the project indicates a broader absence of comprehensive policy and program strategies that address economic insecurity among low-income groups, namely that link phenomena like zero-hour contracts to food poverty and inability to pay for events like funerals.

The third argument is that similarity in the management and designs of social interventions, regardless of area of work or location, allows for comparing responses among practitioners. The responses can include resourcefulness to ensure services exist to address local needs, especially if these needs are not recognized by policy, and to contribute to social solidarity; and opportunism to secure organizational sustainability. Depending on the context, the responses may be analogous across locations or differ because of particular political, institutional, and social factors. Importantly, frontline responses to flaws or gaps in project design influence both the organization and service delivery and use, making the social dimension between policy and practice critical for comprehending how to improve social intervention. The impact can be negative when frontline staff members feel alienated from the methods of intervention.

For instance, investigating practitioner criticism of policy emphasis on skill development and measurement of gender gains in South Africa, Mannell observes that, "Gender mainstreaming itself has become associated with a technical approach to gender issues unable to bring about sustainable change in organisations." The reliance on project management has obscured the experience of inequality and discrimination and thus not addressed what gender means in the practice of social change. She writes:

> Practitioners have placed the blame for the technical approach taken to gender by several organisations across South Africa squarely on any practice associated with gender mainstreaming (e.g. gender-disaggregated statistics, checklists for what gender issues to consider in planning, and tools for gender budgeting), rather than on what might actually be one particular approach to ensuring gender is considered within organisations.
>
> (2012: 426)

Manell captures the general unpopularity of the technical approach in one interview,

> As a practitioner who had been involved in one of the large gender mainstreaming trainings said: It's just been such a horrible experience. So technical. It's no longer about your personal experience. . . . Instead it becomes this horrible technical thing on pages 1–200 of a manual. You've got to fill out all these forms and checklists.
>
> (2012: 426)

In other words, whatever personal motivation the practitioner possessed, it withers under the bureaucratic processes and technocratic language utilized by funding bodies and policymakers. Another practitioner felt that overcoming the oppressiveness of implementing a policy program necessitated concentrating more on consciousness-raising:

> The only way I see gender mainstreaming is going to work is to address consciousness and create activists that can create change in organisations rather than implementing solutions that have been designed by consultants sitting in some office somewhere. Solutions like do x, y and z and then your organisation has been gender mainstreamed.
>
> (Mannell 2012: 432)

Activists had to champion their own knowledge and lived experience, proving its value to those with more education or formally recognized expertise.

The practitioner's call in South Africa for consciousness-raising was evident in the resistance of practitioners in my own research in other locations toward management models emphasizing 'value for money' and the principal-agent relation between government and the voluntary sector. A retired pediatrician in Morocco stated that her medical team, which worked in a public hospital serving primarily low-income patients, "did their job in spite of increasingly difficult working conditions, where human and material resources are reduced to the extreme. We also have difficult relations with the administration." She did note, "It is always satisfying when we can note positive results in an adverse context. Sometimes these results even seem miraculous." For the pediatrician, her supervisors "want to increase the number of patients for the budget without reflecting on the quality of work. How are we going to treat all of these people? Do we have the means to treat them?" She thought public health reform had meant getting rid of doctors while adding managers and clerical staff "who spend their time on computer games and painting their nails. Doctors never meet except to talk about money, which is all the administrators care about."[17]

To compensate for missing care in the pediatric ward, she developed a nongovernmental organization (NGO) to teach the parents of children with Type A diabetes how to care for them at home. This effort was to assert, as she put it, "Public health is a right [though] the state just wants to turn it into charity, the last resort for the poor." Lashing out at the reneging of state responsibility, she exclaimed,

> The administration, like the state, wants social stability. They send us babies born prematurely who weigh one and a half kilos and need equipment and treatments that we just don't have. Rather than speak frankly with the parents about the lack of resources available, they [the administration] prefer to have the children go ahead and die in the hospital. As long as the people don't revolt, they won't change.

Her comment evokes the fourth argument, which concerns the importance of understanding the social experience of frontline work. By experience, this book is referring ultimately to the politics of social action, where frontline staff and managers express social values through their decision-making about resources and activities, their interaction with service users and other local actors like government officials, and their public representation of their work. On an everyday level, the experience of social action, whether individual or collective, can implement or subvert policy and administrative intentions. The choice to reinforce or challenge is based not on Bourdieu's 'objective interests,' but rather a more complicated assessment of opportunities and constraints within the particular environment on how to pursue these interests while conveying values and realizing change (Cohen 2014).

For example, in my research among NGOs in Morocco, the comments of staff in delivering literacy classes suggested that various national programs were not as successful as statistics indicated. As one consultant, a man with decades of experience working for NGOs, summed up, "The state wants writing, reading, and math, in that order, and the women want math, reading, and writing. For women in Berber areas, learning to write Arabic is like learning a foreign language." He then added, though, that the flaws of the policy did not stop organizations from being resourceful with the funding and structure provided to offer the right kind of course to meet needs: "What organizations do is to use the literacy program as a module to create new activities. They work on the literacy program for a year, get to know the social environment better and then do something else."[18]

The manager of the NGO-based project with disabled children, which was funded originally by Handicap International and based in

Sale (next to Rabat, in Morocco), differentiated the values demonstrated in community-based efforts from the incompetence or disinterest of the public sector and government. He had several vocational degrees, one in social development, and was studying for a master's in international relations. He had participated in the activities of the association when he was younger and had continued to volunteer. The manager earned his living working for an agency distributing media but said, "I have time." For him, collegiality, cooperation, generosity, and kindness were critical to making social action effective. He explained, "I have been with AMEJ for many years so I have contributed to the NGO's evolution. When we received the funding [from HI], we decided Hicham [a colleague] would become full-time. He didn't have work and was also very engaged. I will take a job in the future." Though the organization was founded by Mehdi ben Barka, one of the most famous political figures of the post-colonial period, he himself had never participated in party politics because "there were too many problems," and stated: "It is better to be engaged socially." His preference was to continue to work on projects involved in education. "We do a better job of reporting than the government and we hold meetings, we write reports, we are committed."[19]

The fifth argument is that to understand and improve the impact of fields, a conceptual framework must integrate political economy and social theory with approaches to project evaluation. This combination accounts for analysis of contextual pressures on frontline social action and locates the influence of these pressures on what services provide (outputs, in evaluation terminology) and the transformation in quality of life, attitudes, and so on among service users and the wider community (outcomes and impact). More profoundly, the combination reveals breaks in the connections between policy and service delivery and use, concentrating on analysis of the experience of service delivery to show how policy and related institutional behavior, expansion of social networks, and provision of material resources should be altered to strengthen the connection and thus its impact.

In evaluation practice, the Theory of Change (ToC) approach (see Weiss 1997) has a similar logic.[20] The website Theory of Change (theoryofchange.org) states that:

> a Theory of Change describes the types of interventions (a single program
> or a comprehensive community initiative) that bring about the outcomes

depicted in the pathway of a change map. Each outcome in the pathway of change is tied to an intervention, revealing the often complex web of activity that is required to bring about change.

ToC explores where activities and assumptions about outcomes are correct, not complex or inclusive enough of impact, or fall apart and thus need correcting. The national charities evaluation organization in the United Kingdom, Charities Evaluation Services,[21] cites as an example of ToC an evaluation of the Chinese Health Living Centre in London, which was funded through the Partners in Health Programme that was in turn supported by the King's Fund. Initially, the evaluator postulated as her theory that a Chinese advocate with Cantonese and Mandarin language skills would improve access among new arrivals, students, and first-generation settlers to services and increase understanding between clients and health service professionals (Ellis et al. 2011). After investigating the concerns of each group and analyzing the advocate's notes and other documentation, the evaluator refined the ToC to state that the presence of a Chinese mental health advocate with Cantonese and Mandarin language skills would improve access among first-generation settlers, new immigrants, and students to services related to mental health and likewise, improve use of medicine and understanding of medical treatments. The advocate would also increase cultural knowledge among service providers and thus the quality of provision for the community.

The conceptual framework presented here differs from Theory of Change in that it goes beyond the single project to analyze the context in which these projects work and how it constrains their functioning and determines their (at least formal) categorization of the problem and service impact. Likewise, rather than concentrate on the assumptions made about the sequence of intended outcomes within a specific initiative, the proposed approach examines the identification of the problem itself, the assumptions of policymakers in addressing the problem, and the subsequent effects on the design and delivery of practical interventions. For example, I conducted research in Morocco and England with organizations (one in each country) offering literacy programs for women. In both sites, the content and organization of literacy classes reflected political interest in promoting social inclusion for illiterate or non-English-speaking women, government control over service design through mandating a course structure and course content, government funding for the classes, and the delivery of services through community organizations specialized in outreach to women in the local area.

Responding to relatively low literacy rates for a middle-income country and the MDGs, there have been several national programs in Morocco aimed reducing illiteracy rates, particularly among women. When I was conducting research there in 2002–2003, perhaps the most significant initiative was the Alpha Maroc Project, funded by The World Bank with a commitment of $4.1 million (disbursement of $1.2 million) from 2002–2007. According to the World Bank report, the objectives for the project consisted of offering "the poorest adults an opportunity to obtain basic education through high quality, well managed literacy programs" and reducing "the level of illiteracy in the poorest sectors of the working adult population, particularly among rural women and girls" (2008: 1–2). The program was to be implemented in partnership with NGOs "because the NGOs tend to target the poorest population, particularly rural women and girls" (2002: 2). The 2008 assessment report gave the project outcomes a 'moderately satisfactory' rating based on the number of people enrolled in literacy classes multiplying by 2.5 between 2002-03 and 2007-08 and the overall reduction in adult (15+) literacy rates between 2002–2006 from 50% to 43% (2008: 9).

During the research in England in 2007 (after Morocco), English as a Second Language courses run through community-based organizations were being offered to individuals with diverse backgrounds, from highly educated asylum seekers to semi-literate spouses of English citizens. Lacking a coherent government policy and political focus, funding for ESOL was distributed to a range of providers, from colleges to charities. Unlike women and girls in rural areas in Morocco, who were the focus of global and national social policy strategizing, ESOL students in the United Kingdom during the research faced (and still do face) increasing restrictions in immigration policy, such as the introduction of a points system to acquire a work permit. They also confronted (and still confront) antagonism toward immigrants in at least the conservative national media, particularly around competition for jobs but also over population growth and demand for public services (Whitehead 2008).

Though ESOL fulfilled a political aim of making knowledge of English mandatory for citizenship, the government had not made consistent funding for the program a priority. Analyzing ESOL during this period, Roberts et al. remark that ironically

> we have the strange scenario of one government ministry [Chancellor of the Exchequer] advocating that all immigrants to the United Kingdom aspiring to citizenship should have reached particular levels in English, while another [Education] is cutting free provision of ESOL classes for some groups and introducing a user-pays environment.
>
> (2007: 21)

They add,

> there is a persistent need for targeted literacy provision for people with low levels of literacy, but despite greater numbers of teachers trained to teach basic literacy to ESOL students, the time and investment needed for learning of this type is rarely sufficiently resourced.
>
> (2007: 22)

In comparing literacy initiatives in the two countries during the years of research (2002–2007), a couple of points can be made in the relationship between context and service delivery. First, political interest in rural, illiterate Moroccan women benefited NGOs, who could access through offering literacy classes funding and ties with policymakers and international development agencies. In contrast, the weak social status and political capital of non-English speaking women from low-income, migrant communities in the United Kingdom had implications for levels of funding and government motivation. The lack of policy coherence and political motivation contributed to a vicious cycle according to teaching staff I interviewed, who complained that without acknowledging the isolation and marginalization of women in immigrant communities, the classes would not be as effective or efficient as they could be in contributing to a valuation of citizenship. In fact, a consultation commissioned by the Department for Investment, Universities, and Skills recommended that the government focus particularly on 'community cohesion' to improve learning. The consultation recommended retargeting spending "towards those who have made a long-term commitment to live in Britain, rather than economic migrants who may only be here for a short time. In practice this will often mean the most deprived and socially excluded groups who may find it hard to find places on ESOL courses today."[22]

The contrasting political motivations and policy support for literacy programs in the two countries contributed to different decision-making processes, generation of knowledge, and self-identity in social action among staff delivering the courses. The Moroccan organization where I conducted research offered services to women from a primarily rural community. They negotiated perceived constraints in the course length—ten months—and in the textbooks, which they felt did not address the everyday life of the students, by arranging for a volunteer to teach a group of women who wanted to continue. The staff thus secured basic funding for a course the government needed to deliver in order to reach targets on reducing literacy rates while they engaged in more responsive programs without funding. Echoing the comment of the experienced NGO activist cited previously, the director of the women's organization told me,

> We like to think of ourselves as an organization with an agenda. Yet, [with the literacy program] we really are a crisis program. Ten months is not enough to do anything. We have a volunteer who has taken a group of about thirty interested women to continue to study. Her work is outside the state system and therefore not recognized for compensation.[23]

In contrast, the program manager at the organization in Sheffield where I conducted research felt demoralized by the government constrictions on course length and funding limitations and believed she could do little to enhance the program except to allow women to keep enrolling in the same course. The program manager complained that the three-month time limit of her program was "a nightmare. If the program is successful, then people want it to continue. But you can't. If it isn't successful, then you have trouble getting other funding."[24] To make the course effective, she insisted they had to offer a three-month course with classes twice a day to ensure regular attendance.

Instead, the funding for the course at the center provided for one tutor twice a week for ten weeks. Although citizenship required Entry Level 2 English, the organization only had funding to offer Entry Level 1 and none of the women who had taken the course had gone on to the next level at another location. They often began the course possessing little spoken English, though they could understand more than they could communicate. As mentioned previously, they could enroll in a second course at the organization to continue to improve their skills, but this course would include beginners as well, making the level less focused and thus less effective.[25]

The funding for the courses offered by her organization could come from the local government or the local Learning and Skills Council (LSC). The program manager explained that while these funding sources were appealing for voluntary sector organizations desperate for resources, LSCs tended to favor contracting colleges to teach ESOL, "where there are proper systems of education. . . . But we have to bear in mind," she explained, "that many people are more comfortable with community organizations."[26] Community organizations were more suitable for women from immigrant South Asian communities in particular because cultural norms would normally inhibit their going out. "There is a trust issue. You are being encouraged to leave your home. If the program stops, then you have to find something else, but it is hard work."

Her organization received funding from sources like government job centers and adult community learning centers. Unfortunately, they offered "teeny tiny pots of money." Funding, she said, "is all about luck, who you know, not what you know. You need to sell yourself right. If you don't get core funding, then you have to look for little pots of money." Short-term funding not only undermined the possibility of offering effective services, but also created low morale. Employees were uncertain of how the center would fund services and, implicitly, if the center could continue to support their posts. The teacher snapped, "The government talks about embedded this and embedded that, but how can you embed something if you don't know where you are going to be from year to year?"

If utilizing fields of social action as a conceptual framework, then the differences in the responses between the two staff members would be interpreted as going beyond practical capacity to make a difference. More specifically, improving the confidence and morale of staff members seems to depend significantly on national policy interest in the service users, as funding instability, lack of coordination with the government, and other factors appear similar across contexts. Inversely, the actions of the two staff members are linked to how they perceive their social position within their respective political and policy environments, their ability to use their knowledge of the factors that make a literacy course effective in delivering the course, and how they can utilize the contracts to offer courses to further the evolution of the organization.

In terms of evaluation and revising program design, if staff confidence is critical to innovation and service quality, then policy in the United Kingdom should integrate a more articulate discourse of inclusion for immigrants and the role of community-based organizations in offering courses. Instead, policy over the past five years has limited free ESOL courses to those on Jobseeker's Allowance and made the courses fee-paying for those on housing and other 'inactive' benefits.[27] Politicians in the United Kingdom like David Lammy (MP Tottenham) and policy reports have called for greater investment in community-based, perhaps women-only, classes that accommodate family responsibilities.[28] However, beyond more funding, how these courses are taught and the indirect effects of social relations and stronger notions of citizenship and belonging cannot be assumed without understanding the consequences for the teachers and project managers.

Interweaving the five arguments, the rest of this chapter focuses on how a field can be analyzed and assessed, using as a case study an area of work that I have become familiar with over the past few years—interfaith relations. The second chapter discusses why analyzing the relationship between the context and the experience of service delivery is valuable for improving individual initiatives and instigating broader social change. The chapter differentiates analysis of a field of social action from practice-based approaches like 'collective impact'[29] or 'mass collaboration' (Pike 2014), which are deliberately evaluative and prescriptive rather than based on research to generate new ideas. Like fields, these approaches go beyond the single organization, upon which much of practical or academic evaluations are still based, to coordination between initiatives and sectors to address complex problems, like poverty. According to Kania and Kramer, Collective Impact initiatives "involve a centralized infrastructure, a dedicated staff, and a structured process that leads to a common agenda, shared measurement, continuous communication, and mutually reinforcing activities among all participants" (2011: 38). Rather than concentrate on introducing new structures of social intervention, such as the establishment of a 'backbone organization' to support common agendas and coordination, a field of social action is a conceptual framework reliant on research and analysis of the experience of social action to inform better policymaking and, relatedly, distribution of resources, management models, and collection of data. Like 'collective impact,' however, it also looks to understand and challenge segregation of intervention into specific problems and methods of intervention.

Drawing on research conducted in England, Morocco, and the United States, the third chapter shows how comparing fields across contexts can increase understanding of the factors underpinning effective intervention, situate social action in international perspective, and influence global policy and funding agency agendas. The conclusion suggests how fields of social action as a conceptual framework can contribute to more democratic forms of instigating social change.

Research

This book is based on a combination of approximately fifteen years of academic research, three years of teaching evaluation and project management at George Washington University (2001–2004) and practical experience since the late nineties working with community- and faith-based organizations in Washington, DC; Morocco; and Sheffield, London, and Manchester in the United Kingdom. My practical experience includes conducting evaluations professionally or helping organizations to think about evaluation. These projects have ranged from very local, sometimes experimental initiatives, like a parish nursing program in a deprived area of Manchester, to national programs distributing grants to short-term grassroots projects. Overall, I have worked or conducted research with approximately 100 projects, typically conducting interviews with staff and participating, where possible, in activities. I have not interviewed that many service users over the years because of my focus on analyzing how projects are managed and assessed, and in some instances the vulnerability of the service users.

Moving back and forth between teaching or conducting evaluations and conducting research has led me to try to devise a conceptual framework that links conceptual ideas from areas of study like social policy, international development, and social identity under neoliberalism with methods and models of project evaluation. Two experiences in particular, both in Morocco with the same man, a long-term and well-respected actor in the NGO sector, convinced me such a framework was necessary, if only because it resonated with how practitioners themselves thought about their work. The first experience involved teaching a two-week course on project design and evaluation in Rabat in 2003. The man attended the course and at one point mentioned government and aid agency efforts in the southern part of the country to encourage girls living in rural areas to attend school. One policy involved building toilets for girls. "The problem was," he recounted, "was that the boys would sneak in to look at the girls and so they [the girls] would end up going in the field."[30] In other words, policy had not accounted for behavioral responses from all of the actors involved (including the boys at the school) and thus was limited in its success.

The second experience was during a visit he arranged to a rural community organization in central Morocco that was funded by the Ministry of Agriculture. The organization had decided to form cooperatives as the second stage of an experimental project involving training women to cultivate rabbits. When I asked the director of the organization about his strategy for the medium- and long-term, he responded, "The cooperative is our goal." After we left, the well-respected actor turned to me and asked rhetorically,

> What kind of answer was that . . . Cooperatives, why organize cooperatives as an intermediary actor when we have to think about cultivating rabbits? Some technician ran a model and gave it to the organization. Each project at the organization is sponsored by a different ministry and serves expressed needs, not real needs.[31]

Before the visit, I had asked him if people in the region liked to eat rabbit. He had not responded immediately. However, in our discussion after the visit, he told me, "You asked a very good question earlier but we let it drop. You asked if people here eat rabbit. The answer is no."

Posing questions like "Do people in the region eat rabbit?" or "Was building toilets for girls a good decision for increasing enrolment rates?" go beyond figuring out if the project has made the right assumptions, though. These questions evoke more complex issues concerning the choice of rabbits in the first place, the notion of making the cultivation and sale of rabbits a goal of women-only cooperatives, whether or not cooperatives provide sustainable income for the women, and indirectly improve their social position, and why the director had substituted the cooperative for a more profound vision of his organization's future.

Moreover, are these questions relevant to other organizations assisting local women to establish cooperatives? Are similarities and differences between services and how the 'problem' itself is identified due to funding agency or policy initiatives, local government pressures, or other factors?

Through exposure to a range of organizations of different sizes, in different places and often focused on very distinctive areas of work, I have induced the external factors and internal processes, as well as the relationship between the two, which are considered here as influential in determining the choice and quality of social intervention. To offer an example, regardless of country or area of work, 'social networks' have represented a significant factor in distribution of resources and comparative efficiency of service delivery, and thus impact, between organizations. In using the term 'social networks,' I am attempting to convey a structure of power relations with a field, in that staff with longtime experience, well-established organizations, or ideologically aligned policymakers and organization directors share channels of communication, familiarity, and sometimes trust. As I suggest ahead in analyzing interfaith relations, fields with small, tight-knit social networks between policymakers, organization leaders, and perhaps academics may end up with narrowly defined methods of intervention and likewise limited categorization of change associated with participation in activities or services.

Even in fields that are far more expansive and well established, social networks in the research have proven critical for organizations to maintain funding and overcome obstacles. The director of a Washington, DC-based organization serving immigrants from Central and South America, particularly women and families, told me that she used to avoid parties and charitable events because she wanted to avoid the politics of fundraising. Her instinct was to partner with other organizations, especially smaller ones. However, as she stated, "Part of my job is to continue to be collaborative and to continue to bring in the money and sometimes one goes against another." She added, "There almost needs to be a coordinating agency that asks if we are getting a bang for the buck. This needs to be away from politics because all agencies have learned to play the political game." Describing how she overcame her own reluctance to play politics, she related, "With [a former mayor of DC], I said we would do the right thing and not get involved. But he would go everywhere and mention everyone but [our center]. We were out for four years. With the [new mayor], I personally donated to his campaign and worked on a committee for the first hundred days of healthcare. If I hadn't, we would have been out for another four years."[32]

The director of a much smaller community-based organization in Sale, Morocco made a similar comment. A former government worker, he considered networking and exposure critical to securing contracts and grants. He said, "If I haven't heard from someone for a week, I contact them." Access to power through social networks has effects throughout an organization. An education lawyer in DC, perhaps well into his sixties, did not bother with frontline staff in government social service agencies, as he regarded them as insufficiently knowledgeable due to high turnover and lack of education. Instead he sought supervisory staff he already knew to solve a problem. His ability to overcome a potential obstacle contrasted with two young social workers I interviewed at the DC organization working with Latinas, who complained that they had spent hours on the phone trying to speak to government social workers. The difference in contacts may seem logical and insignificant except for the challenges presented to managing human resources, delivering support for service users, and raising the profile of the organization, and thus its capacity to survive.

The exercise here of utilizing ethnographic research to explore management decisions and working life within nonprofit or voluntary sector organizations potentially has more general consequences for the practical value of research and teaching in social sciences. In her account of internationally funded landscape and livelihood projects in Sulawesi, Indonesia (2007), Tania Murray Li is explicitly skeptical of the possibility of combining critical analysis and practice. She argues instead for a distinction between the scholar-critic and the program manager. In one encounter related in her book *The Will To Improve*, she illustrates this distinction and explains her position. After she talks to a program manager about the "troubled history of improvement schemes in the highlands of Sulawesi" (1–2), he responds that "'We can't just give up." She then writes:

> There are always experts ready to propose a better plan. I do not dismiss their efforts. Nor, however, do I offer a recipe for how improvement can be improved. I take a critical stance, one that seeks to expand the possibilities for thinking critically about what is and what might be. I argue that the position of the critic and the programmer are properly distinct. . . .

> Programmers must screen out refractory processes to circumscribe an arena of intervention in which calculations can be applied. They address some problems, and not necessarily others. Under pressure to program better, they are not in a position to make programming an object of analysis. A critic can take a broader view.
>
> (2)

Obviously, in my own book, I am taking a different position. Programmers do not necessarily have to 'circumscribe an arena of intervention' partly determined by the ability to apply cause and effect relations and tag activities with sticky notes of expected results. In fact, many do not do think like this, even if they are pressured to do so in practice. They do so cynically as part of maintaining a reputation or pleasing funding and other partners. The director of the same umbrella body in Morocco that sponsored the training course where we discussed girls' toilets told me once, "A Spanish funding agency just came to me and said we want to include mobile phones for you as part of the grant." Lifting up three mobiles, the director retorted, "I don't need more phones." Yet, he would use the income to support the needs of other staff.[33]

On a more substantive level, project managers and organization directors I have met have persistently tried to innovate, thereby making an existing program an 'object of analysis,' but have been blocked or frustrated by lack of research or conceptual thinking about practice to present to policymakers and funding bodies. For instance, three women I encountered in Morocco (a teacher, a doctor, and a Ministry of Health official who was a longtime friend of both, reinforcing the importance of networks) had received funding for separate projects from the Global Fund through the same Moroccan umbrella organization to run an awareness campaign about tuberculosis and now sought to devise a follow-up project. One of these women, the director of a respiratory clinic in a low-income area of Sale that ran activities for the campaign, had dutifully presented in the Logical Framework—the table outlining goals, activities, and expected outputs, outcomes, and impact—the number of participants the project had stated as the target output figure. Yet, she had also sought from the umbrella organization a more profound understanding of impact that accounted for the poverty and exclusion of TB patients and tracked those who attended awareness events with subsequent diagnosis and treatment. Expressing her frustration with the lack of support in this kind of evaluation, she stated, "There was no chemistry between us."

The follow-on for this project they had conceived centered on providing a basic income to patients. The income would deter TB patients who were still contagious from going back to work and prevent those who were beyond the initial stages of the disease from falling irrevocably into poverty, due to the stigma of the disease and their own mental and physical health. However, though accomplished professionals (medicine and teaching) with experience in charitable work, the three women required not only direct income generation possibilities for a population under treatment but also a policy discourse of inclusion, similar to that of illiterate rural women mentioned previously, and related availability of educational and vocational training resources. In other words, the project leaders needed to take into account policymaker motivation, absent vocabulary and conceptual linkages between income and disease, and the quality of medical care, when conceiving of the project.

Integrating a conceptual framework with improving intervention in the field, so it is more critical of institutional arrangements and power relations, is close to the critical approach to community mobilization championed by academics like Catherine Campbell. Campbell (2014) explains that Freirean materialist approaches have not only had very limited success in marginal communities, instead working better where constituents have more social capital and confidence, but they have also been co-opted by medical agencies to provide new markets for pharmaceutical companies and biomedical services (48). She remarks, "Many of the pillars of the approach (participation, empowerment, agency, and capacity building) have become little more than 'disciplinary technologies.' She explains that these pillars have become methodologies "used by public health and development agencies more concerned with advancing the strategic interests of funders than facilitating social change in favour of the marginalized" (2014: 48). Instead, she wants to 'embed' dialogue between professionals, service users, and the knowledge of marginalized populations "within a wider critical or political emphasis" (2014: 48). She calls for ensuring that projects reflect the economic, social, and political position of the particular community rather than impose a one-size-fits-all model of community participation (CM). She states that CM needs to recognize the "need to develop and apply different theories of health-enhancing change (a) to social contexts which offer different opportunities for survival, embodiment, protest and recognition; and (b) for different types of social struggle (e.g. struggles for physical health vs. struggles for social respect)" (57).

The conceptual framework outlined here is arguably a 'technology,' though inherently reflexive about context and how to create, in Campbell's words, a "receptive social environment." Analyzing fields of social action provide a mechanism for overcoming flaws in theories of change adopted by funding bodies, governments, and practitioners alike by altering the environmental pressures that sustain these theories. Developing a 'technology' may appear to support those with control over resources rather than challenge them, but as Bob Deacon notes in criticizing the approach of leftist scholars like Hardt and Negri (2000), who want solutions to come from the masses, "while 'waiting' for the posse to get its act together, we should seek to reform existing neoliberal global capitalism in a global reformist direction" (Deacon 2007: 191).

Though beyond the scope of this book, connecting research and conceptual thinking to practice could also inform teaching. Most of the discussion around public sociology has been led by Michael Burawoy, former president of the American Sociological Association and a professor of sociology at the University of California, Berkeley. Burawoy strives to legitimize the effort of public sociology rather than lay out an explicit agenda of what public sociologists are supposed to do in their work. Zussman and Misra (2007) speculate that his 'vagueness' is deliberate, an "expression of long-standing utopian traditions meant to set free the imagination" (7). Burawoy focuses instead on fighting for the legitimacy of public sociology in an academia molded by tenure battles and financial pressures. He warns that opposition to public sociology within the discipline, particularly by those in elite universities, "will confine public sociology to the state universities and colleges, thereby stigmatizing its practitioners as second-class citizens. Public sociology will be labelled second-rate sociology" (2005: 388).[34]

Burawoy predicts that public sociology will eventually move beyond policy consultation (second wave) to engaging directly with 'publics' or forms of teaching like service learning within organizations. However, his discussion of service learning concentrates on the academic experience rather than impact outside the university. He pushes sociology teachers to acknowledge the multiple dialogues occurring between the trained sociology instructor and the student participating in the training, between students, and between the student (and often the instructor as well) and the communities or other groups with whom they are engaged (2007: 254). Similar to the challenge posed to research and critical thinking, service learning could go beyond data collection for organizations and the difficulties Burawoy associates with it as a form of training, namely when the organizations "become more demanding, calling on sociologists to service their immediate needs, subverting their autonomy, and pushing them in a policy direction" (2007: 254). Instead, service learning could offer training in critical reflection, critical approaches to community mobilization, and social innovation based on research. Deriving better practice from conventional academic fields of study like political economy would not fall into 'applied research,' which Orlando Patterson claims (2007) sociology departments have "rejected," such that "no major department will today consider hiring anyone, however distinguished in their own right, who works in applied areas such as social work" (182).

Analyzing a 'Field'

The creator of Theory of Change as an evaluation model, Carol Weiss, writes,

> Theory-based evaluation is one approach that has a great deal of promise. But trying to use theory-based evaluation is difficult when programs do not have any explicit—or even implicit—theories, when programs are amorphous, or when they shift significantly over time. Foundations and governments will exert pressure on evaluators to develop new ways of evaluating these complex multi-sector programs, and the need to answer harder questions will force us to develop new approaches.[35]
>
> (1998: 1)

She adds, "Evaluators should view themselves as part of an ongoing enterprise to develop knowledge for action" (1998: 1). Arguably, going beyond program evaluation would be part of this enterprise.

The field of interfaith relations in the United Kingdom offers a potentially useful case study for exploring evaluation where programs do not have explicit, or implicit, theories and initiatives are 'amorphous.' For example, Interfaith Week, a national government sponsored initiative run annually in November by the Interfaith Network,[36] states as its aims (a) 'strengthening good interfaith relations at all levels;' (b) 'increasing awareness of the different and distinct faith communities in the UK, in particular celebrating and building on the contribution which their members make to their neighborhoods and to wider society;' and (c) 'increasing understanding between people of religious and non-religious beliefs.' Broad aims like 'good interfaith relations at all levels' make it hard to associate the activities of an interfaith initiative with indicators of impact, especially if the latter is not explicitly defined in terms of specific changes in relations.

Faced with the ambiguity and idealism of interfaith activities, the few studies that have addressed evaluation of interfaith initiatives have focused more on describing the initiatives (see Abu-Nimer 2004; Neufeldt 2011; Thorley 2007) than on case studies of impact. In her report on evaluating interfaith initiatives, Renee Garfinkel comments, "So far there has been very little research on their effectiveness. This is unfortunate, because those who design and implement interfaith programs need feedback to determine how to maximize their efforts and resources" (2004: 9). Six reasons explain the failure of a relevant body of evaluation research: (a) the politicization of interfaith relations at a national and local level; (b) the dependence of many initiatives on the founder, which can affect motivation and capacity to evaluation impact; (c) the lack of project design and designation of specific aims in interfaith initiatives; (d) the diverse, context-driven, and subjective nature of interfaith initiatives, both within and between locations; (e) the challenge of using a cross-national framework to understand how initiatives alter knowledge, attitudes and behavior among participants and the wider faith communities to which they belong; and (f) the absence of training for interfaith initiative staff to conduct internal evaluations or even gather data on their activities.

Furthermore, as stated previously, evaluation approaches for assessing health, social, and education projects are made possible because of cross-national policy agendas (like the Millennium Development Goals) and extensive knowledge transfer among governments, NGOs, and funding agencies. Both cross-national policy and knowledge transfer benefit in turn from an extensive international body of research on the effectiveness of projects. These projects can range from the fairly straightforward (like health immunization campaigns) to the complex (for instance, a women's empowerment project that incorporates education, legal services to ensure rights, and microfinance to support economic independence). In circular fashion, they are all based on the project design-expected impact framework that policymakers and funding agencies recognize as the basis for evaluation and thus utilize when developing new, ostensibly more effective, policies and programs. In contrast, interfaith initiatives are not guided by a comparable international policy agenda, and thus cross-national coherence in project design and aims, and are not evidence-based because the literature does not exist.

In addition, the significance of context for understanding impact and the lack of rigorous design among initiatives pose difficulties for using existing academic and practice-based evaluation methods. These methods are generally applied to health, education, and social projects and 'test' the effectiveness of a project's design in achieving its stated aims. Academic evaluations often rely on a comparative evaluation framework to assess effectiveness. For instance, they can analyze the attitudes and behavior of service users before and after participation or compare participants with a control group of non-participants. Academic evaluations can also utilize randomized selection of individuals who have used a service to determine if there are generalizable effects from participation.

Comparing service users and non-participants raises another difficulty in applying methods used for health and social projects. Participants in interfaith initiatives are typically motivated to learn and change, negating the value of making comparisons with non-participants—who may be far less motivated to change—in order to gauge the impact of the intervention. Randomized selection is more possible, but again, the choice of this methodology obscures the role of motivation in changing attitudes and behavior. The most motivated and active participants may have the greatest influence on transforming perceptions within their respective faith communities.

I suggest that analyzing interfaith relations as a field to assess and improve its impact overcomes these challenges and complements concentrating on the evaluation of a single project. In analyzing a field of social action, Carol Weiss' remark about the difficulty of evaluating projects without clear logics of intervention, or causal assumptions between activities and effects, would also become a question about the context. What does the absence of desired and measurable outcomes within projects in interfaith relations say about the origins of these projects? Who are the actors that have invested in the field, and what are their relations with each other? What is the connection between policymakers and other elites and the 'frontline' of interfaith activities?

Weiss calls for 'meta-analysis' and building a 'stock of knowledge,' though her intention is to devise methods for evaluating individual programs. Similarly, when evaluators like Debra Rog or Jennifer Greene mention context, they generally relate it to the setting of an evaluation of a single initiative, where the question could be how the context should influence the choice of evaluation method (Rog 2012) or how evaluation can account for the particular ethnic and cultural environment (Fitzpatrick 2012). In a description of context in evaluation, Greene (2005) writes, "the setting within which the evaluand (the program, policy, or product being evaluated) and thus the evaluation are situated. Context is the site, location, environment, or milieu for a given evaluand" (2005: 83).[37] Sensitivity to context is required to avoid value judgments or exclusion of relevant information for assessing an intervention and its effects. Fitzpatrick remarks, "U.S. evaluators, who are primarily from white, middle-class, educated backgrounds, have recognized that their own personal contexts and values influence how they see, or fail to see, other cultures. As such, our evaluations are invalid" (2012: 14).[38]

Context regarding fields of social action instead refers to the behavior and decision-making of relevant institutions, policymakers, and philanthropists or charitable funding bodies in an area of work and how relationships between the three actors determine distribution of resources, capacity to become sustainable and grow, and impact among the nonprofit or non-governmental organizations within the field. These three interrelated effects of the environment augment the prominence and power of certain organizations while constraining, directly or indirectly, the possibilities of others, a process that establishes a public profile and expectations of a field and ultimately underpins its reproduction. As suggested above, contradictions at the level of service delivery can undermine reproduction by raising questions about impact and relevance, in turn pushing funding bodies, policymakers, and institutions to decrease support.

The aim of devising a conceptual framework is for scholars, evaluators, practitioners, and service users to have more influence over the relationship between context, range of activities, and impact—and more generally, the reproduction or transformation of fields and thus process of social change. Thinking through a field can focus attention on the characteristics of the internal structure of the field and the range of activities, including the theory (or theories) of change, of intervention. Which organizations are the most established, well funded, and integrated into political networks? Which organizations struggle financially and/or are unstable? What are the characteristics of the organizations that are well funded—are they typically large or fit into a niche area of service provision? In contrast, which organizations are not sustainable—are they small or medium-sized, local, and/or resource-intensive?

Comparing the mission statements, activities size, and funding of a sample[39] of organizations involved in interfaith relations in the United Kingdom suggests that regardless of differences in size, scope, and resources, interfaith relations as a field is characterized by two related methods of intervention to achieve more positive engagement: religious literacy to promote greater understanding and self-confidence in the presence of other faiths and establishing 'neutral' forums that bring together members of representatives from different religions and/or denominations. The assumption inherent to forums is that platforms, whether in academic, educational, religious, or other settings, will encourage open discussion and self-reflection and thus engender greater understanding and mutual respect between participants. The desired long-term impact is improved relations between the wider faith communities due to changed perceptions among participants and sharing their experience with friends and family networks.

Interfaith relations as a field of practice emerged from theology and religious studies. Theologians like Wilfred Cantwell and Martin Buber emphasized the necessity of listening to the 'Other' and taking seriously the beliefs and existential meaning inherent to other faiths (Buber 1937; Cantwell 1981). The 'I and Thou' relationship conceived by Martin Buber particularly influenced the format of interfaith forums. He emphasized that authentic communication, in which the participants hear what each other says, has no institutional or ideological framework. He wrote,

> The relation to the Thou is direct. No system of ideas, no foreknowledge, and no fancy intervene between I and Thou. The memory itself is

transformed, as it plunges out of its isolation into the unity of the whole. No aim, no lust, and no anticipation intervene between I and Thou. . . . Every means is an obstacle. Only when every means has collapsed does the meeting come about.

(1937: 10–11)

Prefixed ideas, prejudices, or the historical legacy of encounters should not interfere in the actual, lived, immediate encounter.

Consequently, interfaith forums may be sponsored by a particular institution, like the Church of England's Lambeth Jewish Forum, or an organization, like the Fethullah Gulen movement's Rumi Forum, but the physical encounter is organized deliberately to foster perceptions of openness and equality. For example, the mission of the Rumi Forum (founded in 1999) is "to foster intercultural dialogue, stimulate thinking and exchange of opinions on supporting and fostering democracy and peace and to provide a common platform for education and information exchange." It achieves this aim through "conferences, panel discussions, community engagement, luncheons, publications, and other activities."[40] Similarly, The Richmond Interfaith Forum (Southwest London) is sponsored by the local council but the forum itself is "a platform for local people from different belief groups to meet up and discuss issues of mutual interest. The aim of these discussions is to make recommendations to local agencies, based on equality and inclusion."[41] The only exclusionary clause is to show "respect towards others and a focus on mutual understanding and action. The Forum is not a platform for theological debates, extremist views, or for undermining any religion or belief."[42]

Some organizations involved in interfaith relations in the United Kingdom, like The Interfaith Network, state simply that they work to promote understanding, cooperation, and good relations.[43] Faiths Forum For London "empowers religious communities to work together for a better London,"[44] and London Faiths Borough Network states that it is "an active, informal network of people from local religious and intercultural groups." This network shares "experience and expertise in working with public agencies (borough councils, police, NHS) to make a positive impact on the lives of our local communities, particularly those who rely on public services."[45] The Muslim-Jewish Forum in Manchester offers more detail, declaring as its mission: "To educate members of the

Muslim and Jewish Communities in relation to their shared values and common Abrahamic tradition, heritage, history and culture; and to promote better understanding within the wider community of our common interests and values."[46]

Other interfaith organizations cite as their justification racism, conflict, and sometimes, violence. The British-American organization Coexist states on its website: "Globalization has outpaced understanding, creating divisions that plague societies with prejudice, misinformation, hate, and violence." The organization works in "communities with a history of conflict" and its theory is that "by creating opportunities for people to work and learn together we help build relationships, knowledge and common purpose to advance coexistence."[47] 3FF (Three Faiths Forum), which focuses on religious education in schools, makes a similar argument:

> In our diverse societies good relations between our communities are essential. Without these ties, myths and prejudices flourish, often leading to racism and intolerance. Our programmes break down barriers and find ways for people to work together to improve their communities and society. By building new intercommunal relationships we make positive social change possible.[48]

A significant part of 3FF's work is in secondary schools, training teachers and students about religious diversity and overcoming tensions. In describing its work in education, 3FF states that it teaches understanding of different faiths and beliefs as well as internal diversity, dismisses myths and stereotypes, helps young people to ask questions that respect the sensitivity of others, and finally, gives students an opportunity to learn more about their own faiths and share their experiences with others.

A few initiatives, like the Ariadne de Rothschild Fellowships or the Near Neighbours Programme,[49] integrate interfaith relations with another field, in these cases, social entrepreneurship and social action. Most of the time, however, forum activities involve different approaches to achieving religious literacy and, within this, occasionally a specific method called scriptural reasoning. For example, forums can celebrate together different religious festivals, meet to discuss common issues or differences, or educate each other on the tenets, practices, and internal diversity of the other faiths. Scriptural reasoning represents a more academic version of this education process. According to Jeffrey Bailey (2006), it is the

> group study of scriptural texts from the three Abrahamic religious traditions. At any given meeting, with roughly equal numbers of each faith represented, passages from the three scriptures are read. A theme (say, debt relief) usually relates the texts together. A few introductory comments about a scripture passage are made by a member of that faith, and then the entire group attempts to understand what the passage is teaching, and how it ought be applied to today's context.

However, though the general theoretical premise, aims, and activities are similar substantively across projects, organizations themselves can differ dramatically in their scope and resources. The field includes academic, local, practice-based, and national umbrella organizations that are connected through networks and occasionally partnerships or memberships in umbrella bodies. These initiatives have different access to funding, policymakers, and religious leadership, and each other, creating a field with distinctive areas of sustainability and others that are far less stable and consistent. Local interfaith forums are volunteer-based and their activities may include public multi-faith celebrations, dialogue to discuss specific political or theological issues, or meetings to discuss local concerns or tensions regarding interfaith relations. The Crawley Interfaith Network declares as its objectives "encouraging an atmosphere of goodwill and peace between different faith communities, promoting an attitude that reflects on commonly held beliefs leading to the acknowledgement of differences and celebration of diversity, and inspiring understanding and respect between faith groups."[50] Its purpose and work involves providing "a means for the general public to be involved in multi-faith activities," "an initial contact point whenever there is a need for consultation or assistance on multi-faith issues," "arranging annual/regular activities, including events open to the general public, which are religious, cultural and social gatherings," and creating "dialogue to support bridge building amongst faith and secular communities in and around Crawley."

In contrast, The Interfaith Network and Faith-based Regeneration Network receive funding from the Department for Communities and Local Government (DCLG); in addition to member fees, 3FF has received funding from a number of private foundations, the City of London, and the British Council; and The Cambridge Interfaith Programme, situated within the University, has received funding from private donors, particularly from Oman and the United Kingdom. Both Coexist and 3FF have worked with the Cambridge Interfaith Programme, located in the Faculty of Divinity at the University of Cambridge. Focused explicitly on scriptural reasoning as a method, CIP's mission is to explore within Judaism, Christianity, and Islam "the different resources that each faith has for serious engagement with each other, and with the wider secular and religious context." CIP's work with 3FF involves a scriptural reasoning project with hospital staff in Israel of different faiths and with Coexist, a number of leadership training and cultural projects.[51] In addition, Coexist and CIP share donors and staff members.

These partnerships reveal the characteristics of the context that have helped promote and sustain the position of organizations like these within the field and likewise, their shared emphasis on religious literacy as a method of improving interfaith relations. Expectedly, members of churches and other religious institutions in the United Kingdom are important actors in setting up local interfaith forums. They also offer public support for national networks and organizations, such as The Council of Christians and Jews, which was established by the Chief Rabbi and Archbishop of Canterbury in 1942 to combat racism and intolerance and is one of the oldest interfaith organizations in the United Kingdom. However, it is government and private philanthropic funding that has contributed more significantly to the development of service providers within the field and a structure of internal diversity and opportunities for growth and impact. This funding expanded considerably after the 9/11 terror attacks in the United States but with the imposition of austerity measures after 2010, organizations that rely largely on private philanthropy and project grants have maintained their activities whereas organizations dependent on government support have struggled (such as The Interfaith Network of the United Kingdom) or closed down.[52]

The latter, which include quasi-governmental faith councils (like the East of England Faiths Council), have not been replaced, leaving a small number of service-providing organizations with a national profile and a greater number of local, largely voluntary, and low-budget interfaith forums to form the structure of the field.

To illustrate differences between the two types of organizations, 3FF, Coexist, and CIP have all received substantial endowment funding from individual philanthropists that has enabled them to remain stable while seeking funding for particular projects (CIP also benefits from its integration into Cambridge University). For all three organizations, these projects are largely educational and cultural in orientation, including, as mentioned above, training of teachers and faith education in school for 3FF and summer schools for religious leaders that are managed by CIP and Coexist.

Inversely, the eleven-member (in 2014) voluntary executive team of Muslim-Jewish Forum in Manchester is composed (with the exception of one member) of local Muslim and Jewish activists in interfaith relations and its annual budget for 2013 was £3,806.59. Its primary activities include celebrating religious festivals and organizing interfaith dialogues, talks in schools, trips to mosques and synagogues, and international tours, such as to Israel and Palestine. Other forums, such as the Leicestershire Interfaith Forum, are not funded but are supported logistically by the Leicestershire County Council.[53]

Faiths Forum for London has a larger number of voluntary members (twenty-six), primarily religious leaders, than Manchester's Muslim-Jewish Forum but is not consistently active. As one local vicar noted, "Faiths Forum of London is a kind of representational body and its capacity to do work is limited." London Boroughs Faith Network is more dynamic as a network of local interfaith activists. Yet, as the same vicar pointed out, even this Network has suffered because of the cuts. He explained,

> At one point there were a lot of interfaith forums. This has diminished because of the funding. It's not just the funding. The previous government was really into the notion of faith communities working together and they thought, all the sort of spin was they could impact hard to reach communities. All that was understood is that they had a bit of power. It is certainly completely out of fashion now except for Near Neighbours.[54]

Policy thus had a significant influence on both participation in interfaith dialogue and the expected impact of dialogue.

In addition to analyzing mission statements, funding, histories, and activities across organizations, assessing a field entails examining contradictions and correspondence in the experience of service delivery across a range of organizations and projects, from those in the mainstream of service delivery (like 3FF) to those on the margins, whose work falls within the same area but diverge in terms of activities and missions from conventional projects. In 2013–2014, through several different research projects, I interviewed approximately twenty-five local activists in interfaith relations, clergy, and program staff involved in interfaith work. I asked them about public and local motivation to participate in interfaith work and the impact and sustainability of interfaith activities, and how they would alter the work of interfaith relations to improve both. Their responses revealed both problems for the current status of the field and provided the basis for transforming it through rethinking the practices that would generate better understanding and relations and, inherently, challenging the founding principles, such as neutrality of venue.

For instance, one project manager of an interfaith employment project noted that they attracted youth not because of the interfaith element but rather the opportunity for training. The subsequent friendships or increased familiarity with other faiths was a consequence but not necessarily a motivation. In fact, activists in interfaith relations often mentioned how younger generations lacked interest in interfaith relations, perhaps because of growing disaffection with religion, assumption of diversity, or other priorities. A Catholic activist in North London stated flatly, "I don't think I have had any impact on young people at all. The only event that attracts them is the Westminster Interfaith Peace Walk (in June)." He was positive about his overall impact, having engaged in interfaith dialogue for decades after colleagues at the library where he worked posed questions about his faith. He said,

> I have got a lot of people together. I have improved communications . . . I have very patiently built up my group at the cathedral. I had a meeting the other week and thirty people came up to me. I have become known. I wanted to put on the map that the Catholic Church is very committed to interfaith.[55]

The activist did note that Muslim communities were particularly reticent about interfaith work, perhaps because of the internal power structure. "If you take Finsbury Park or Streatham Mosque, it is the same group that holds power. The founder and his family have to agree to change. Younger generations that want to initiate change seem to be waiting for the older generation to die off." Other difficulties facing interfaith forums included the mobility of the London population, where "You can't maintain a consistent group of participants. . . . Any religious organization has a mobility problem. For example, a thousand people attend a service Saturday evening but maybe there are fifty congregants."

Forums also faced lack of available funding, particularly since 2010 when the coalition government took power, and limited interest among religious leaders who faced internal challenges within their own communities, from declining membership to polarizing theological debates. He remarked, "Leaders all know each other and getting them to an event helps. It puts a public face on interfaith work. We also have to face the fact only a few leaders are interested in this." He did qualify this critique, though, adding, "Lay people are encouraged to get involved but have no authority. . . . But interfaith is about people meeting and working together, so authority not an issue within a group dynamic." His description of the obstacles facing interfaith forums was echoed in interviews with many of the activists, though local clergy and program staff of community- and faith-based organizations often expressed outright cynicism or more polite skepticism about their value. When I mentioned to a young vicar in Tottenham, one of the most diverse areas of London and site of the 2011 riots, that I was going to see Rowan Williams, then the Archbishop of Canterbury, give a talk about interfaith relations, he retorted, "Why?" His view was that interfaith relations occurred when he walked out the door of his parish church. Another vicar, who occupied a relatively senior role in the church in London regarding social action, categorized interfaith relations as an important academic exercise, away from the daily experience and needs of individuals and communities.

Some senior religious and lay figures have lamented the decline of interfaith forums or, like the local vicars, attributed their waning popularity to their negligible contribution to improving interfaith relations. One of the most well known scholars of faith and social action in the United Kingdom, Adam Dinham, has referred to interfaith dialogue as "A pragmatic cobbling together of people who already want to work together" and commented that the Labour government policy discourse of "Face to Face/Side by Side policy discourse went entirely without comment," showing that interfaith dialogue as an exercise "responds to policymakers more than lived reality."[56] For Dinham, without committed leadership, buildings, and basic tenets, forums only attract those already deeply motivated on a personal level and cannot engage individuals who reject communication with other faiths.

A former high-level figure working in the Lambeth Palace, the home of the Archbishop of Canterbury, admitted in an interview that, "interfaith relations are not the same kind of priority for the Church of England now that it was with predecessors."[57] For him, the current Archbishop, Justin Welby is interested in interfaith relations when applied to specific issues, like relief work. He also told me that, "If you have two projects, one to clean up a park and one to understand each other better, I would bet on the park." However, for this priest, the trend did not mean that interfaith relations no longer represented an issue. He commented that government funding for grassroots multi-faith projects, channelled through the Church Urban Fund's national program Near Neighbours, "have a social action aspect, but what is suffering are the dialogical aspects of it. You know, about getting along better." Reflecting on the consequences of rejecting interfaith work, he remarked, "What I am hearing from Birmingham is that multi-faith forums are not coping. They haven't been able to provide the kind of leadership necessary. For example, Birmingham Faith Forum is not really active. They probably did have some money at some point and may still meet occasionally." Reflecting on the future of interfaith work, he did believe that "There is a new generation coming up. I was at a Sikh forum last night and none of the traditional participants were there. That was interesting to me. Younger leaders were taking things into their own hands. They work cheek by jowl with people of other faiths."

The dynamism of the Sikh forum as opposed to the decline of the Birmingham Faith Forum could be attributed to the appeal of the single-faith platform or the absence of traditional leadership. From an evaluation perspective, if only government funding or the commitment of older volunteers can maintain the presence of explicitly interfaith forums, then these types of forums need a new logic of intervention. I suggest, though, that the challenge to the theoretical basis of interfaith dialogue goes beyond a Theory of Change approach, which focuses on correcting false assumptions and remaking activities to achieve the aims of the initiative.

Conceptually, local clergy and lay leaders made a connection between expression of their own religious identity, the manifestation of their faith's values in practice, and benefit to others. In other words, the encounter between faiths or with individuals of no faith combines theology with social idealism, egalitarian politics, and concrete action and is deliberately lateral and grassroots. Increasingly interfaith encounters at a local level are not dependent on government interfaith funding or decision-making among religious or political leaders. In fact, mutual suspicion of the state and institutional leadership often provides the basis for focusing on how religious identity and individual and collective social contribution intersect. This association reflects a different understanding of civic engagement and even citizenship than the contribution of public service used, for example, by Gordon Brown in his resignation as a Member of Parliament:

> Sometimes politics is seen at best as a branch of the entertainment industry. There are times when political parties seem not to be agents of change but brands to be marketed to people who are seen as consumers, when they are really citizens with responsibilities.[58]

Instead, the rhetoric is of transforming public and private institutions to respond to the singularity of individuals and groups, to use the terminology of French philosopher Pierre Rosenvallon (2013), while ensuring access to necessary resources across the population. The obligation of citizens is to mobilize locally for each other, or to work to provide support and respect for other groups that may differ religiously, economically, and socially but reside in the same area. For example, criticizing cuts to housing benefits and more general caps on benefits for working families,[59] the director of an organization serving the Orthodox Jewish community in North London commented:

> In policy, the language is that you have too many kids so you are a drain. They want to remove the child benefit after two kids. But that is an intrusion into private life. Who are they to say how many kids you should have? It's the idea of a drain. What about our contribution? There is no weighing up.[60]

Their contribution, to her, was to provide services that could be replicated in other communities or were used directly by other local area groups. In a similar challenge to authority, a local vicar stated,

> What is really needed is not a question of the church hierarchy making statements. It is a question of our having grassroots community organizations engaged together in a way that shows that within communities there are people who care and they have got power and that elected politicians realize it is important to listen to them or they will be exposed to risk themselves.[61]

Though Christian in its origin, the effort would only succeed if it attracted members of other faiths within the same area. He noted,

> More community organizing, more church engagement in community organizing to influence wider society, that is the model that is going to bring about change and that is very much an interfaith model as well, working with people of all faiths and none.

However, for him, this influence would only come about from connecting the practice of community organizing to theorizing a different social role for the Church as an institution. He explained that the church was

> moving in a positive direction, but largely what we are about as the Church of England is gathering people together to serve their kind of needs. When we talk about reaching out, what we are talking about is growing our church. There is a lot of evidence that one of the features of growing a church is to be socially engaged.

Yet, he stressed,

> What is really required is a theology of social engagement that is ... about what we are about as Christians. That is one of the positive things about this austerity period, churches have gotten their hands dirty ... people have not been doing stuff but have started to think this feels like real Christianity. This gives me the opportunity to make connections, what society is like, how do I relate to it, how do I share love.

Likewise, for community-based religious and lay leaders, tensions in interfaith relations could not be overcome through structured 'neutral' forums but rather through sustained communication between members of different faith communities who understood how institutions and social networks in other communities operated. The important knowledge was not therefore just theological but also political and social. An Orthodox rabbi with years of experience in cultivating relations with the neighboring Muslim community in North London related how the two communities avoided tensions through responding quickly to incidents and calling in relevant clergy to speak to the involved parties, who would be encouraged to apologize or make necessary amends. The result of this familiarity with hierarchy and influence was a cultivation of trust and desire for stability that superseded external pressures, such as a crisis in the Middle East. The director of the Jewish organization, who worked in a nearby area to the rabbi, told me that her son had heard a story of a young boy who was assaulted and hospitalized by two Muslim youth shortly after the 2014 Israel-Gaza war. She insisted, as did others in the community, that it could not be true. Indeed, the story ended up being of a young man being insulted verbally by an "Asian-looking" man in the West End of London.[62]

The disaffection with traditional forums of dialogue, which are characterized by processes of learning about the other in neutral venues, and the shift to improving relations through social, political, and institutional knowledge of the Other, challenges the original theological foundation of dialogue outlined by Buber. In an era of austerity and expanding far-right politics, local interfaith initiatives are changing to focus on joint mobilization of local resources or single-faith provision for the wider community. These efforts likewise indirectly or explicitly make claims upon policy, institutional behavior, and structural processes rather than respond to government or religious leadership directives, even if projects like food banks or credit unions receive political support.[63]

Interfaith activities thus counter critiques of religious institutions that they lack the historic radicalism that influenced, for instance, the creation of the welfare state in Britain[64] or that social action has become a substitute for interfaith dialogue and a bandage for problems like hunger that obfuscates structural inequality and exploitation. In a debate on religion in the House of Lords (November 27, 2014), Lord Parekh claimed that

> When we talk about the great work that religions do, we always think of charitable activities, which look after the victims of our society. I have long

waited to hear the radical voice of religion. . . . The radical religious voice which tries to transform the economy and the social structure is rarely heard. It is striking how, in a liberal democratic society such as ours, religion can easily be co-opted into an ameliorative function, looking after the victims of society but not challenging society itself. We need to be very careful when we talk about faith-based action. We tolerate faith-based action as long as it looks after the victims of society, but if it takes the form of radical challenge, such as occupying Wall Street, or whatever, we begin to think very differently.

(*The Hansard*: Column 1015)

The perception of lack of radicalism could be that within grassroots interfaith relations in highly diverse areas of London, or even cities more segregated by faith like Leicester, manifesting faith or beliefs is not about conventional politics but rather the effort to realize subjective principles in local social change. The 'interfaith' dimension of this effort is the necessity of understanding both the subjective meaning of social change within other faith or non-faith groups and their own means and methods of achieving it. As the Catholic activist cited previously said, "Talking is great, but action is very important."

Transforming the field thus involves responding to contradictions between frontline service delivery and the context, including policy, institutional behavior, and access to resources. This response entails (a) rethinking the theoretical and philosophical ideas that have informed design, management, and evaluation; and (b) integrating these ideas with a new approach to practice that addresses characteristics of the field like the sustainability of a particular type of organization or the range of diversity in service design. For instance, in reflecting on interfaith initiatives, the effort to demonstrate faith or beliefs to others could be interpreted as the 'living will' that Emmanual Levinas, a philosopher-theologian, highlights when analyzing the work of another Jewish theologian Franz Rosenzweig (1990). Levinas writes that Rosenzweig wanted an alternative interpretation of the individual's position in history to that of philosophers like Hegel (or Marx), where the "the significance of a work is truer in terms of the will that wished it into being than the totality into which it is inserted . . . the living willing of will is indispensable to the truth and understanding of the work" (1990: 200).

Engaging theoretical ideas should not be beyond the work of practitioners and applied research, as this engagement prevents obscuring often ideologically driven assumptions within policy about individual behavior, inequality, social obligations, and so on. Thinking theoretically also allows for critiquing language, such as 'service user,' which again neglects the critical importance of social relations to the quality and effectiveness of intervention (Oxfam 2009; Cohen 2014). What constitutes 'theory' may differ by field, for instance interfaith initiatives are derived from theological and philosophical analysis. More importantly, negotiating the relationship between ideas and practice diminishes the boundary between the two, as the two forms of knowledge, academic and practical, respond to the other.

Redesigning interfaith activities that go beyond neutral forums and religious literacy could, if premised on encouraging the effort or subjective will to instigate change, emphasize promoting cooperation reflective of the challenges posed by the context and the status of relations between particular faith groups. Raising the need for neutral forums to cultivate relations of difference, in *I and Thou*, Buber argues that "No system of ideas, no foreknowledge, and no fancy intervene between I and Thou. . . . Every means is an obstacle. Only when every means has collapsed does the meeting come about" (11–12). However, he also writes that relations between I and Thou develop in the present, and that the present is "continually present and enduring. The object is not duration, but cessation, suspension, and breaking off and cutting clear and hardening, absence of relation and of present being" (12–13). These terms evoke the dynamics of forming, disrupting, and re-forming specific relationships.[65]

Following this latter comment of Buber's, interfaith work directed at cultivating the will to achieve change and the particularities of attitudes and behavior in a singular place and time would become more fragmented and localized, but at the same time more reflective of both diversity in interfaith relations and current disaffection from forums. Adopting a flexible, contextualized approach to interfaith work, in which some initiatives offer religious literacy because they are located in areas where faith communities are segregated and others assume knowledge and thus stress other areas of work like public institutional reform and rights, may increase not only practical impact but also the public presence of the values of openness and respect the field represents.

In practical terms, if this transformation of the theoretical and practical dimensions of the field of interfaith relations occurred, it would become less hierarchical in its organization and more adaptive in its activities and conception of impact, though an open-ended aim could be determination and expression of common values. Indicators of impact would subsequently change and in principle, initiatives would become more dependent in funding on community mobilization of resources. The field would become less dependent on political interest at an elite level but perhaps more invested in politics and inclusion in policy, particularly around freedom of religion and belief, reform of public institutions, and accessibility of benefits and support for the members of the faith community and residents of the wider area. The point, though, is not how the field would change specifically, as this would be result of the work of stakeholders like local activists, academics, policymakers, and religious leaders (similar to collective impact, mentioned previously, in setting up a committee to discuss and oversee collective evaluation). Rather, it is that the field can and often should evolve into an arena more effective for generating the kinds of social change people at a grassroots level want.

Conclusion: Social Action and Democracy

In *Religion of the Future* (2014), the Brazilian philosopher Roberto Unger argues for a doctrine he calls 'deep freedom' which "combines a devotion to the empowerment of the ordinary person—a raising up of ordinary life to a higher plane of intensity, scope, and capability—with a disposition to reshape the institutional arrangements of society in the service of such empowerment" (342). He calls for "a trajectory of institutional change designed to support what it describes as the higher forms of cooperation. More than any particular way of organizing society," he writes, it is a movement "toward a structure that organizes its own revision." Becoming increasingly impassioned, he adds that individuals must question and reorganize those institutions and practices on a personal level, despite the probability that they will see little of the desired change in their lifetimes. The focus of this revision must be transforming the organization and representation of social relations:

> Whatever our view of the road to our ascent may be, it must be expressed in the terms of our relations to one another: not just the way in which we

choose to deal with other people, in the small coin of personal encounter, but also the way in which society is organized in the large currency of its institutions and practices.

(2014: 342–3)

Trying to understand how to confront challenging social problems in an era of political stagnation and incapacity, Gilbert (2014) writes that methods like participatory budgeting "enable the 'governed' to engage more directly, deliberatively and continuously in the process of decision-making than do systems based solely on parliamentary-style representation."[66] This book analyzes how institutions, and associated political ideologies, policies, and management models organize social action and social change. Inversely, the book shows how examining and revising specific interventions and more general conceptions of social problems and social impact challenge the social role of institutions and the nature and direction of policymaking, as well as funding streams. Furthermore, prioritizing the knowledge and motivation of (non-elite) service workers and users provides a basis for reflexive and active citizenship that must, within the approach outlined here, rely on communication, cooperation, and coordinated grassroots mobilization to influence policy. From a policy perspective, a framework like a field of social action compels policymakers to adopt a more comprehensive and responsive approach to identifying and defining problems and devising strategies.

Notes

1 Bourdieu and Wacquant define field as "a network, or configuration, of objective relations between positions" (1992: 97).

2 Swartz adds, "Indeed, Bourdieu's concept of field should not be reduced to the neo-classic idea of market. Rather, the concept suggests a force-field where the distribution of capital reflects a hierarchical set of power relations among the competing individuals, groups, and organizations. Interactions among actors within fields are shaped by their relative location in the hierarchy of positions" (1996: 79).

3 The World Bank defines empowerment as "the process of increasing the capacity of individuals or groups to make choices and to transform those choices into desired actions and outcomes. Central to this process are actions which both build individual and collective assets, and improve the efficiency and fairness of the organizational and institutional context which govern the use of these assets." http://web.worldbank.org/WBSITE/EXTERNAL/TOPICS/EXTPOVERTY/

EXTEMPOWERMENT/0,,contentMDK:20245753~pagePK:210058~piPK:210062~theSitePK:486411,00.html

4 www.unitedway.org/our-work/education/

5 www.hfrp.org/evaluation/projects/family-engagement-for-high-school-success

6 www.hfrp.org/evaluation/projects/family-engagement-for-high-school-success-completed-project

7 Ibid.

8 www.lematin.ma/journal/2014/eradication-de-l-analphabetisme-le-maroc-a-tout-pour-y-parvenir/199892.html

9 www.unesco.org/new/fileadmin/MULTIMEDIA/HQ/ED/pdf/Maroc.pdf

10 See, for example, www.glassdoor.org.uk/nightshelter.htm or www.wlm.org.uk/what-we-do/westminster-churches-synagogue-night-shelter

11 For example, The Salvation Army states that it offers "Advice, signposting, recreational activities and individual key work appointments. Some clothing. Hot meal during Wednesday drop-in 5.30–8pm. Service users can call in any time during opening hours to make an appointment. Advice and enquiries Mon, Tues, Weds, Fri 2.30pm-4pm." http://advicelocal.org.uk/advicefinder/london

12 www.shelter.org.uk

13 www.quakersocialaction.org.uk/Pages/Category/down-to-earth

14 www.gov.uk/funeral-payments/overview

15 www.goodfuneralguide.co.uk/2013/12/regulated-funeral-industry-look-like/. This may be changing through lobbying Parliament.

16 www.dailymail.co.uk/news/article-2543006/The-rising-cost-dying-Average-funeral-costs-7-600-thousands-struggling-afford-fitting-send-off.html

17 Interview with pediatrician, June 13, 2009.

18 Interview with NGO consultant, July 15, 2003.

19 Interview with NGO volunteer, October 5, 2009.

20 ToC can apply to both complex and relatively simple projects. In contrast to the Chinese Healthy Living Centre example, which is based on the presence of a support worker with the right skills, The Hunger Project (www.thehungerproject.org.uk), listed as an example on the Theory of Change website (www.theoryofchange.org), has nine activities and a wide range of expected changes in access to services, advocacy and knowledge, government behavior, service quality, and income. The ultimate goal is sustainable, vibrant, healthy rural communities free from hunger and poverty.

21 www.ncvo.org.uk/practical-support/consultancy/ncvo-charities-evaluation-services

22 www.dcsf.gov.uk/readwriteplus/ESOL_consultation

23 Interview with program manager, March 11, 2007.

24 Interview with program manager, March 11, 2007.

25 An evaluation by the National Institute of Adult Continuing Education found that: "In fact, in an evaluation of ESOL courses, NIACE recommends that local [Learning and Skills Councils] make the provision of Entry Level 1 and 2 more coherent. Guidance to local LSCs should make it clear that Entry Level 1 and 2 provision leading to nationally approved qualifications is fundable, and that one of

the objectives of their purchasing strategy for ESOL should be to achieve a balanced portfolio of provision with clear progression routes available for learners."

26 Interview with program manager, March 11, 2007.

27 www.learningandwork.org.uk/sites/niace_en/files/document-downloads/ESOL%20policy%20update%208%20Sep_0.pdf, www.gov.uk/government/uploads/system/uploads/attachment_data/file/297859/ESOL_joint_DWP_SFA_note_and_QA.pdf

28 See the All-Party Parliamentary Group on Race and Community report on ethnic minority female unemployment (Runnymede Trust 2012), pp. 4–5.

29 See www.fsg.org/publications/guide-evaluating-collective-impact

30 As an aside, seven years later an employee at the national umbrella body for local NGOs, which had sponsored the course, told me that she had heard of the toilet example in a meeting outside the office, explaining that both the course and this example has developed a lasting reputation.

31 Though not a funder of this project, the International Fund for Agricultural Development (IFAD) proposal does mention "The local administrative structures of the Ministry of Agriculture and Rural Development will assist cooperatives in formulating development plans, mobilizing the required financing, and implementing them" (IFAD 2003b: vi).

32 Interview with director, January 7, 2009.

33 Interview with director, July 2, 2008.

34 Burawoy largely favors a critical sociology that simultaneously challenges the insulation of the professional discipline from the public and likewise, offers the knowledge and skills of professional sociologists to a more general public. He defines public sociology as "a sociology that seeks to bring sociology to publics beyond the academy, promoting dialogue about issues that affect the fate of society, placing the values to which we adhere under a microscope" (2004: 104). He separates these publics into a "thin, passive, and national" public that reads newspapers like the *New York Times* and expresses interest in a 'traditional' public sociology of op-eds and articles, and a second grassroots public responsive to an 'organic' public sociology. This sociology carries "sociology into the trenches of civil society, where publics are more visible, thick, active, and local, or where indeed publics have yet to be constituted" (2004: 104).

35 www.hfrp.org/evaluation/the-evaluation-exchange/issue-archive/evaluation-in-the-21st-century/interview-with-carol-h.-weiss

36 See www.interfaithweek.org.uk/

37 She identifies five specific dimensions to context in evaluation: demographic characteristics of the setting and the people in it, material and economic features, institutional and organizational climate, interpersonal dimensions or typical means of interaction and norms for relationships in the setting, and political dynamics of the setting, including issues and interests. Her identification of five dimensions of the contexts of evaluations is an important contribution to our beginning to think about context in a comprehensive, systematic fashion (2005: 83).

38 She adds, "They become invalid in many ways: by identifying the wrong questions to frame the evaluation, by ignoring key stakeholders who are potentially strong users of the evaluation, by misinterpreting stakeholders' priorities or even

program goals, by collecting data with the use of words or nonverbal cues that have different meanings to the audience, by failing to describe the program accurately or to understand its outcomes because the evaluator is unable to notice nuances or subtleties of the culture, by reporting results in means only accessible by the dominant culture or those in positions of power, and so on."

39 This comparison was done through interviews and analyzing documentation, whether online or print.

40 www.rumiforum.org/about/about-rumi-forum.html

41 www.richmond.gov.uk/inter_faith_forum

42 Ibid.

43 See the homepage of Interfaith Network at www.interfaith.org.uk

44 www.faithsforum4london.org

45 http://lbfn.org

46 www.muslimjewish.org.uk

47 www.coexist.org/about

48 www.3ff.org.uk/about-us/

49 www.adrfellowship.org

50 www.crawleyinterfaith.net/management/

51 www.interfaith.cam.ac.uk/publiceducationprojects/projwithcoexist

52 The Interfaith Network and Faith-based Regeneration Network both receive funding from the Department of Communities and Local Government.

53 www.leicestershire.gov.uk/about-the-council/equality-and-diversity/religion-and-belief

54 Interview with priest, November 14, 2013.

55 Interview with Catholic lay leader, January 18, 2015.

56 From a March 4, 2014 lecture entitled "Assessing the Impact of Interfaith Activities: Part Two," Westminster College.

57 Interview March 2, 2013.

58 www.theguardian.com/politics/2014/dec/01/parties-should-not-be-brands-says-gordon-brown-announces-quitting-parliament

59 Shelter, the housing and homeless charity offers clear information on benefit reforms—http://england.shelter.org.uk/get_advice/housing_benefit_and_local_housing_allowance/changes_to_housing_benefit/housing_benefit_changes_2013

60 Interview February 5, 2014.

61 Interview with vicar, April 22, 2015.

62 Interview with director on February 5, 2014.

63 www.dailymail.co.uk/news/article-2864772/Welby-faces-food-banks-backlash-Archbishop-calls-state-war-hunger-MPs-say-feckless-parents-waste-cash-cigarettes-drink.html, www.independent.co.uk/news/uk/politics/food-banks-archbishop-of-canterbury-urges-politicians-to-face-up-to-britains-hunger-9909324.html, www.churchofengland.org/our-views/home-and-community-affairs/home-affairs-policy/work-and-the-economy/creditunions.aspx

64 http://williamtemplefoundation.org.uk/modern-welfare-state-william-temple-church/

65 See also Vollmer, Hendrik (2013). *The Sociology of Disruption, Disaster, and Social Change*. Cambridge, UK: Cambridge University Press.

66 www.opendemocracy.net/ourkingdom/jeremy-gilbert/common-ground

CHAPTER 2

ASSESSING THE CONTEXT OF SOCIAL ACTION

A long-term volunteer for a Sheffield-based project in the United Kingdom that arranges for adults to accompany young people (ages ten to seventeen) detained by the police explained how he thought project management had altered over the years. He was one of the first volunteers in the country for the Appropriate Adults Scheme, a nationally mandated service launched in 1984 that functions locally through either statutory sector agencies or voluntary sector organizations. During his twenty years as a volunteer in Sheffield, responsibility for delivering the service had passed from the statutory sector to a large national charity to a medium-sized voluntary sector organization. The volunteer told me that he thought the nature of the crimes themselves, for instance, burglary and motor crime, for the most part had not changed; even the number of violent crimes and crimes involving drugs had not increased. He noted that perhaps he saw more repeat offenders, which he conjectured meant the offenders were serving shorter sentences. What had changed for him was the management of the project. He thought each agency had demonstrated distinct volition and capacity in providing an effective service.[1]

He was bitterly critical of how Social Services, where the Scheme originated, had managed the project. However, as I will discuss ahead, he did think that the project belonged under the authority of the state. He told me that when Social Services ran the Scheme, the project manager depended on three adult volunteers for all youth arrests in Sheffield. The volunteer alone did 450–550 call-outs a year out of a total of about 1,200. He received £10 for expenses for each call-out. The volunteer recalled,

> It was the most disorganized Scheme in the world. Out of every day, there were two or three calls a day sometime. . . . Nothing ever seemed to get done. Social Services really weren't bothered about what the service was. You went out three times with an Appropriate Adult, and then you were an Appropriate Adult.

Eventually, the government contracted the project out to the local chapter of a large national charity working with children.[2] The charity managed it for three years, making a few changes in project management. The charity introduced training and monitoring forms and the project manager expressed more interest in how Appropriate Adults acted during police interviews with youth. "In the early days, we spent a lot of time arguing with the police about how to conduct interviews. At [the charity], during the last bit, the manager didn't like the police." Despite the changes, though, project management remained fairly lax and detached. To the volunteer, the charity had pursued the contract simply for the money and thus had not adequately prepared either for the substantive work or the costs entailed in managing the project effectively. They had bid for the contract with a £11,000 budget ("They way underbid"), leaving them with funds to hire one part-time worker, "Which was way under what they needed."

The volunteers benefited from the shortage of management in that they could assume individual initiative with cases. Left without guidance on the weekends, the Appropriate Adults could talk directly to emergency social workers about cases. The Appropriate Adult volunteers could build relationships with individuals to discuss the circumstances of a particular young person. The converse of such freedom was that the project manager, with his scarce resources, could do little to take advantage of such relationships and process any information passed on by the volunteers for improving the project. The volunteer commented, "Any information you were feeding back wasn't getting to the right people."

After the charity's contract expired, the Youth Offending Team re-issued the tender. A new organization won the contract and instituted tighter management procedures.[3] The project manager taking over the project adopted a less confrontational approach with the police and implemented more regulation of interaction with the public sector. The new rules regarding paperwork and volunteer contact with social workers limited individual initiative but did allow for processing their feedback. Rather than call social workers directly, volunteers now had to fax the project manager the information and wait until Monday until he could respond.

The volunteer believed that they were "the best people to work for." The organization had more office staff and the manager read every form and looked into every concern. The volunteer stated, "You know that something will be done with the information collected (from the volunteers)." The organization required more training than the other agencies, inviting police to conduct mock interviews with potential Appropriate Adult volunteers. They also dropped a contract with a private firm that the previous charity had used for calling volunteers to attend a police interview. Rather than go down a list, the private firm would call those volunteers known to be generally available. The volunteer received a lot of phone calls. Instead, the new organization asked the police to make the calls and the police used all the names on the list.

Regardless of who was managing the Scheme, for the volunteer, the intervention of an Appropriate Adult for youth in detention did little to address the social problem: young people, generally from marginalized (low-income, ethnic minority) communities, facing arrest and insertion into the penal system, often not for the first time. He blamed the government for how it managed the service, whether directly or indirectly through contracting, and for failing to bring together all of the actors involved in the welfare of the individual young person. He mentioned having found one youth sleeping on the floor at a friend's unbeknownst to Social Services, who thought he was still with his family. "They should know that to help him." Because of his own lengthy experience, he could contact emergency duty officers directly to expedite a response to a case. The officers would respond positively because they knew him and because "The emergency duty team likes to be in the know before a crisis happens." Furthermore, he could find out what happened to the youth he helped because police officers and solicitors would tell him, whereas the organization would not.

For the volunteer, public sector contracting for the service inevitably pushed organizations to concentrate on presentation of management.

This effort perhaps detracted from time spent reflecting on the social aims of the service or how to support appropriate adult volunteers. He complained that,

> I got about as much thanks from Social Services as I do at [the new organization]. You don't do it for thanks, but you occasionally need something. I was once invited to a do at the town hall because they realized I had been working as an Appropriate Adult for twenty years. Our appreciation party is a trip to the pub. But I think that is not right. The managers should get together and put together our sandwiches. They should not send out a form letter but write a letter themselves.

He continued with a broader criticism of the organization's priorities,

> I think [the new organization] is getting bigger and has started to forget volunteers who do the work for them." He noted that "Like [the first charity], [the new organization] did not ask any of the Appropriate Adults how the project worked. I think it is a matter of seeing £40,000 or whatever it is, and they go for it.

The volunteer's reflections on his experience as an Appropriate Adult indicate the range and number of factors that make a service effective. Government policy interpretation of the problem, or its separation from the life experiences of young people in custody, and the decision to deliver the service through contracting charities, in effect segregating it from public sector agencies, affected impact. The volunteer's criticism of the lack of information flowing between agencies dealing with the same individuals, namely Social Services, the penal system, and charities, indicated how much policy had cordoned off the issue of unaccompanied minors facing arrest from more profound intervention to alter behavior.

The other factors influencing the effectiveness of the service were primarily relational, or the network of support for young people who were arrested, including social workers and families, and the interaction between the police and the Appropriate Adult volunteers and between the organization running the project and the volunteers. In fact, his stress on relationships predated a 2016 report from the British Probation Inspectorate, which found that supportive professional and personal relationships and interventions designed to facilitate daily activities were the most effective means of preventing re-offending.[4] The volunteer also noted the significance of the quality of training for volunteers, which reflected on how the organization treated the project, the number of motivated and dedicated volunteers (he did this despite a family and a stressful, high profile day job), and how the program manager treated the volunteers.

This chapter asks how project design, implementation, and evaluation should address the combination of external factors influencing the delineation of the social problem and related needs and effective delivery of the service. The question has implications for the data collected to establish and assess a service as well as its management. Much of what the volunteer narrated would be regarded as 'anecdotal' evidence concerning the functioning of a frontline service. Yet, to reconsider the impact of a program like Appropriate Adults, should not the relationships—including depth of cooperation and not just communication—between the government and relevant frontline service providers be integrated into more formalized approaches to project development? Considering these factors would also reveal whether or not the program itself, and thus government policy, should change, most likely to become part of a more comprehensive approach to desistance among young offenders.

For the volunteer, the project represented crisis management, not a social service. Speaking in 2009, when the Labour government was still in power, he remarked,

> The Labour government has put it [the Appropriate Adult Scheme] out to tender. It is a quick fix [the project]. To actually properly fund the program with MSWs [social workers], it might cost £200,000. If you look at the total budget of a place like Sheffield, you would think they could pay for it.

He personally favored a scheme in which Social Services assumed responsibility for special cases, perhaps multiple repeat offenders. "In some cases, you know that things are not going to change," he said. He argued:

> The service might be better in the public sector with qualified social workers who would have to take responsibility for what people are telling them. For example, you hear that there are a lot of youth in trouble. When they give you their home address and you call and you find that they are sleeping on a friend's floor. It may take a week to ten days for a social worker to find

them and they are gone because they don't want to go back to their parents. This would all be more direct if their information was in the system. Now, an Appropriate Adult shows up, but if the statutory sector participated, something could be done.

Finally, the volunteer criticized government focus on management and how it affected operations within the voluntary sector. "I think sometimes smaller is best. These organizations are getting big on management and that is the reason I think [the new organization] will lose it. And if you lose one project, it is like a house of cards."[5]

Following on from the volunteer's criticism of the service to which he had dedicated so much time, this chapter explores the potential for developing an alternative approach to social intervention, and by necessity policy. Rather than concentrating on the internal stages of designing a project or building internal capacity, the chapter asks how social problems within a particular context become identified by different actors, how these actors respond in designing services, what social and material resources they access to deliver the service, and how together, project design and available resources affect social impact and wider organizational decision-making. The chapter looks across a number of examples in different locations to analyze how social action reflects opportunities and constraints generated by the political, institutional, social, and economic context. At a macro level, what effect does the context have on social relations among different actors and the types of services and the size, sustainability, and other characteristics of organizations addressing a particular problem? On an organizational level, how does the context influence service innovation and internal decision-making about allocation of resources and strategy?

Rethinking Social Intervention

A service depends upon identifying a need related to an underlying problem, such as hunger generating a need for available food or indebtedness creating a need to pay off creditors, and then addressing it through providing regulated access to resources, from food banks to debt advice. If managed and used properly, these resources can be linked to tangible indicators of impact. The textbook *Designing and Managing Programs* (Kettner et al. 2008) refers to four types of 'needs' service developers should consider: normative, expressed, perceived, and relative. These categories translate multiple perspectives on a social problem into the features of health and social services. For example, a literacy program for older women incorporates the normative need of learning to read and write, the expressed need of demand for such a program, the perceived need among potential service users of what literacy can offer, and the relative need(s) of different sub-groups of service users, such as older women or recent migrants.

In another example, the American national mentoring partnership organization, Mentor, views the need for mentors as children lacking relationships with supportive, encouraging adults. This lack affects self-identity and specific decisions about friends, education, health, and jobs, in turn affecting life chances. As a responsive service, 'Responsible mentoring' is "a structured, one-to-one relationship or partnership that focuses on the needs of mentored participants."[6] The mentor provides caring and experience for the mentee/young person, who responds by becoming more engaged with school and avoiding behavioral patterns that would lead them into crime, poverty, and/or drug addiction.

The equation between increasing access to a methodically organized service and the decline of a well-defined problem facilitates using procedural approaches like 'best practice' to create new programs, increase impact, and guide performance expectations both among staff and beneficiaries. For instance, the Mentor handbook *Elements of Effective Practice for Mentoring* (Garringer et al. 2015) lists six core standards of practice, including recruitment, screening and training of mentors, matching with mentees, monitoring and support, and ending the relationship (2015: 5). Benchmarks are the practices needed to meet the standards. These practices are based on evidence of effective mentoring relationships and maintaining the safety of mentees. Enhancements are additions that can increase effectiveness but are not required. While some organizations may apply benchmarks differently, depending on their existing model, the handbook emphasizes the importance of possessing a theory of change in setting up a mentor program, noting that, "A good theory of change should [i]llustrate how the program's work is designed to explicitly bring about change [and] [e]xplicitly show how a program, through the work of a mentor, achieves meaningful and measurable results." Finally, it should demonstrate the "validity of the program design and how the services align with local needs, contexts, and circumstances."(8)

This chapter inverts the order of components of a 'good theory of change,' concentrating instead on how the context influences the understanding of the social problem, service design, organizational characteristics and decision-making, and impact. With the context in mind, the chapter examines project aims and categorization of 'need,' types of available services, and existing external and internal constraints on organizational capacity to address the more extensive social problem; for instance, why young people commit and continue to commit crimes. Organizational capacity can depend upon access to political networks, current policy directions, and sources of funding. Inversely, these constraints can affect the kinds of organizations that enter and survive in the field and the services they are able to offer.

By examining the influence of contextual opportunities and constraints on organizations and the development and delivery of services, the approach encourages devising ways to maximize the former and overcome the latter in designing more effective, most likely comprehensive, services. For example, a revised Appropriate Adults Scheme could bring together volunteers, mentors, police, related charities, and social workers to discuss the welfare of particular young people and devise strategies to prevent re-offending, including strengthening stable relationships and knowledge sharing about living conditions; invest more in volunteer appreciation to ensure long-term commitment, saving the costs both of training and mistakes made because of lack of experience handling sensitive situations; and include regular meetings with relevant local and national policymakers.

Just as project design might be affected by relating identification of the social problem and need to the organization and the context, so may the definition and analysis of social impact. Instead of referring to impact as the changes the particular intervention generates among individual beneficiaries–such as a child, through a continued relation with a mentor, graduating from school and attending a university–impact would be wedded to sustaining or transforming the organization and the context. If desistance among young people depends upon strong, supportive relationships, then in addition to the development of these relationships and not re-offending, impact may include the survival of small organizations offering intensive, person-centered services, as desired behavioral changes would not happen without the sustainability of particular providers. Impact would also refer to regular, constructive communication between relevant government agencies, such as Social Services and the Probationary Service, educators, families, and employers, if appropriate, so that individual progress is monitored and any needs addressed. In other words, the context itself would be an object of analysis, making service providers, policymakers, and other actors responsible for achieving change.

Analyzing Constraints in the Context for Social Intervention

The American historian Michael Katz warns against substituting a single factor for the complex social and economic conditions that produce a 'social problem,' in the case of his argument, citing family life as the cause of poverty in the United States. He writes, "A focus that lingers on ghetto poverty distracts attention from its sources in transformations of social structure that threaten the well-being of a very large share of Americans" (1995: 87). On a far more local and concrete level, a staff member at a Citizens' Advice Bureau (CAB), the nationwide network of agencies offering information and advocacy support in the United Kingdom,[7] once complained to me about how policymakers conceptualized need.

> They think in terms of funding organizations that offer services to the elderly *or* funding organizations helping youth and children. What they do not think of is the mother who comes into CAB with young children *and* an aging mother. We miss out because we do not fit into a category of funding.[8]

The two quotes underscore the consequences of singling out one area and occluding related issues as well as the context in which the issues are situated, whether of inequality or dependency, due sometimes to lack of affordable private care or available public services.

Analysis of 'constraints' has figured into research and theories of project management in business. G.K. Rand (2000) describes the primary components of the Theory of Constraints posited in the first of Eli Goldratt's novels *The Goal*:

> 1) Identify the system's constraint(s); 2) Decide how to exploit the system's constraint(s); 3) Subordinate everything else to the above decision; 4) Elevate the system's constraint(s); 5) If, in the previous steps, a constraint has

been broken, go back to step 1, and do not allow inertia to cause a system's constraint.

(2000: 174)

Rand offers as an example of constraint a bottleneck in production,[9] where a particular machine is impeding overall capacity to meet demand and thus needs to have its own schedule, perhaps to be in continuous operation.

Investigating constraints on social intervention means examining how external factors impede effective intervention in an area of work, including how the social problem is defined. Are these factors structural (for instance, the prevalence of flexible work contracts in low-skill jobs undermining the ability of job placement or related social interventions to have sustainable impact)? Is the impediment institutional isolation that hinders or prevents the necessary communication between stakeholders?

Research on how the context affects nonprofit and voluntary sector organizations has concentrated on the influence of the community or neighborhood on organizational characteristics and sustainability (Galaskiewicz 1997; Lincoln and Miller 1979; Audia et al. 2006). For instance, the analysis of Vermeulen et al. (2014) shows how the level and kind of embeddedness within neighborhoods influences the survival of immigrant organizations in Amsterdam. In their study of Turkish, Moroccan, and Surinamese organizations, those with a religious affiliation or a diverse board of directors, among other characteristics, could access varied resources, including from the particular immigrant community (18).

Christopher Marquis, in a number of different papers (Marquis and Tilcsik 2013; Marquis and Battilana 2009; Marquis et al. 2007; Marquis and Huang 2010), has looked at the concept of 'imprinting' to understand how external factors influence organizations. With his co-authors, he outlines a process of 'imprinting' that consists of "brief sensitive periods of transition" that begin with "high susceptibility to external influences," followed by the entity coming "to reflect elements of its environment" and finally, "the persistence of imprints despite subsequent environmental changes" (2013: 2). Imprinting as a conceptual framework "helps researchers pinpoint when history matters" and "serves as a powerful tool to systematically identify significant but often subtle contextual influences across levels and over time" (2013: 57).

The population ecology approach also examines the influence of the context on organizational sustainability and change (Baum and Oliver 1996; Baum and Singh 1994a, 1994b). The approach primarily correlates exogenous structural factors, such as the geographic density of organizations, with specific empirical trends; for instance, organizational survival and innovation (Twombly 2003) or fiscal efficiency among community foundations (Guo and Brown 2006). In his study of the effect of AFDC (Aid for Families with Dependent Children, which preceded Temporary Assistance to Needy Families in the United States) waivers on the survival of human service organizations, Twombly argues that environmental conditions, like new funding arrangements, that hinder the entrance of new organizations may in turn "suppress the formation of new and innovative groups that could more effectively address the needs of local residents than existing nonprofits" (2003: 232).

As mentioned in Chapter 1, impact evaluation typically acknowledges the influence of environmental conditions on implementation and the choices made in designing and conducting the evaluation (Fitzpatrick 2012; Fitzpatrick et al. 2004; Lopez 2005). However, the frequent aim of evaluation and principles of 'best practice' are to prioritize learning across projects, and contexts. The Kellogg Foundation evaluation manual calls for using evaluation to "provide important information about general principles of effective practice. . . . These types of findings can be used to collaborate, share, and learn across programs and initiatives with common themes and principles" (1998/2004: 101).[10] Beyond practical evaluation models like Collective Impact, which brings together different stakeholders as part of the evaluation process, and thus partially alters the context, it has been unusual to prioritize analysis of the context within evaluation methods. Concentrating specifically on relationships and communication in an area of work, Rick Davies has written extensively on utilizing social network analysis to understand how interaction between different stakeholders affects impact. He writes, "Social network analysis (SNA), and specifically the use of network diagrams and matrices, is an important potential alternative to the Logical Framework. . . . All development programs involve people and relationships, operating at different levels of scale and formality" (2009: 1). He argues that, "Network diagrams and matrices can describe those actors and their relationships in terms which are easy to understand and possible to verify" (2009: 1).

This information complements data on service users; for instance, relationships may perpetuate or challenge destructive behavior and attributes (2009). Importantly, mapping networks of relationships between service users and service providers allows for understanding how communication and coordination across relevant actors, or lack thereof, affects the achievement of project aims and offers a more realistic depiction of service delivery than a linear model focused on how activities within one organization and program generate outputs, outcomes, and longer-term impact. For Davies, recognizing the significance of relationships makes more actors accountable for change and clarifies division of labor as well as overlapping responsibilities and shared or distinctive priorities (2009).

Focusing first on the context would necessitate going further than mapping social networks to investigate how the quality of relationships and communication, and the factors impeding them, affect capacity to address the complexity of individual circumstances. On a daily, practical level, like the volunteer in the Appropriate Adults Scheme, voluntary and nonprofit sector staff have often explained to me how they relied upon contacts in public sector agencies to manage their cases. They, in turn, received calls from their public sector counterparts asking for help. For example, the director of a church-based organization based in Sheffield that supports older people told me in 2008, "I have social workers—a couple who specifically work in this area—who ring me and ask me if I can go visit 'so and so.' They cover such a big area that they don't have time."[11] In interviews conducted in 2009, two young caseworkers at a center supporting Latino immigrants to the Washington, DC area laughed at how much time they spent waiting for a welfare agency employee to pick up the telephone.

In contrast, during the same research trip,[12] a lawyer based at Georgetown University with decades of experience explained that since he knew the supervisor's number, he could try to resolve quickly cases of denial or termination of benefits so as to avoid legal action. Similarly, the director of the Sheffield church-based organization explained that

> Because of contacts that I have, if I can't get something fixed through someone I know—my weakness is BME [black or minority ethnic]—but generally, if someone comes to me with a problem, if I can't fix it, I can find someone who can.

Other organizations in my research have had regular communication with the relevant public sector agencies through seconded staff or sharing local offices. For example, a Sheffield-based program that worked with young people currently or recently in government care happened to be located in a social services building. The program manager had worked in social services for years and was significantly older, and more experienced, than her colleagues working in the public sector in the same building. She told me in 2008, "I am perhaps in a better position than most because I am in a Social Services building." She also added that because of her experience, the social services staff looked up to her as a leader and source of information.

Inversely, sometimes communication can be so poor as to inhibit the delivery of a service. In a 2004 interview, the manager of a high school mentoring program in Washington DC described his relationship with the school system as "frustrated necessity."

> We just beat on doors all the time trying to get the kids out. We start noticing there is a problem, failing courses, in November but it is too late to get any real meeting before Christmas and then the semester ends in January and then you finally get your meeting in March. They say, "Yeah, there are about seventy absences." Insane things like that.
>
> You go to parent-teacher meetings and it takes five conversations to find out who is the guidance counsellor and you say you are the counsellor and they say, no I don't think so, you should talk to this person. We say no she said talk to you. And he looks it up and says oh yeah, sorry, I haven't had a chance to meet her. I only meet those who are failing. And you say, she is failing five courses. So we get their attention but there is zero follow-through. That is basically our relationship with the school system.

Similarly, a project manager at a community center in Sheffield stated in 2007, "We used to have good relations with people in Social Services but that is not happening anymore. It is hard to find anyone. We have a good relationship with the police. Social Services, no. You can't find anyone." He added that he could not fathom why the public sector resisted cooperation. "Look how much service we offer for nothing. We tend to do overtime and a lot of tasks that we are not paid for. If we are not here, then who is going to do them?"

Though important, avenues for communication and cooperation in delivery should be analyzed in combination with other contextual factors like funding and policy, which affect organizational characteristics, capacity, and impact. For example, community-based organizations coping with the effects of welfare reforms under austerity in Britain often possess good local networks among government officials, health practitioners, and other charities, particularly Citizen's Advice Bureaus, which can help on a range of issues like public benefits and debt, and Job Centres. At the same time, conditionality on welfare benefits has arguably significantly constrained the ability of these organizations to assist low-income families and individuals, who are often facing a set of issues like disability and lack of work experience. Sanctions enforced because of behavior, such as missing a meeting at a Job Centre, stop the distribution of benefits, disrupting, sometimes dramatically, the income stream for individuals often already unable to pay bills (Watts et al. 2014; Dwyer and Wright 2014). Other punitive measures include stopping Employment Support Allowance[13] because the individual is deemed 'fit for work,' and the bedroom tax on social housing, which requires payment for unused bedrooms. The latter can particularly affect vulnerable families unable to find alternative housing quickly enough after a room becomes free.[14]

In my research on community-based responses to austerity in England from 2014–2017, directors and staff of local food banks, community hubs for support services, credit unions, and other organizations, often referred to sanctions, the bedroom tax, and stoppage of ESA payments as the immediate causes of using their services. For example, the director of a food bank in East London related the story of an older couple that had lost their son at 26 who was severely disabled. He told me, "they were hit with the bedroom tax [on extra rooms in council housing] a month later. The loss of benefits meant that he hadn't eaten for five days to make sure his wife with diabetes could eat." He added that they "both have mental health issues, so triple whammy—lost son, sanctioned, and struggling themselves." The wife had called in tears asking about food, saying, "I have eaten but my husband hasn't." The director remarked, "you wouldn't believe it unless you saw it, seeing more and more tragic situations, situations shouldn't be happening in a first world country in the 21st century." In an interview, the director of a café for low-income mothers in Coventry that offers a number of public health, nutrition, and skill development classes asked me, with a hard look, "Do you like sanctions?" She went on to describe several cases, one of a woman whose husband had been hit by a bus and was left brain-damaged and without use of his legs. The woman had missed appointments at the Job Centre and so was sanctioned. Another woman had come to the café who had pawned her phone to feed her children.

More than reliance on emergency services, sanctions affect the ability for programs to make a significant difference to individuals, as any progress could be undermined by sudden loss of benefits and the appeal process. The latter is often successful but leaves welfare recipients without public support until the initial decision is overturned (Webster 2013). Therefore, even if the social problem addressed by community-based charities can still be categorized as poverty, the various interventions to address it, like offering classes to develop skills or support groups to low-income single mothers, can be as much about overcoming the consequences of government policies as they are individual circumstances. The understanding of the 'problem' these organizations are addressing should arguably be widened to include fair access to benefits, and the investment in resources to manage individual cases should be recognized in project design and evaluation.

A project in a deprived area of Manchester helping young people to resist offending indicates how a combination of contextual factors can limit the scope of project design, constrain organizational capacity, and lead to a misrepresentation or misunderstanding of impact. In this case, those factors include the social distance between local residents and the local government, which was reinforced by regeneration policies that appeared managerial and self-serving rather than responsive; the lack of communication between local leaders, sometimes with criminal backgrounds, and the police; and scarce resources generated antagonism between, on the one hand, the project's founder and trustees and, on the other, relevant government officials. The context inevitably reproduced the gulf between residents with criminal backgrounds or tempted to commit crime and the government, inhibiting the potential of the project to instigate the wider change among young people in the area the founder envisioned. The problem itself was inevitably not just the possibility of offending or re-offending but also the absence of cooperation across the different actors, which any intervention needed to address.

The project consisted of a gym and office space for small businesses at the back of a Methodist church, which the founder director attended. The project differed from that of the services offered by the local authority in that it targeted youth with criminal backgrounds, even those continuing to commit crimes. The director attributed delinquency among youth to disconnection from public institutions and family breakdown, and likewise the attraction of gang life. The theory behind the center was that these youth could, through activities like belonging to a gym and physically maintaining the center's building, change their behavior. The newly confident and socially aware youth would then influence youth still unengaged in crime to stay out of trouble. In essence, the director was arguing that if a social project could reach the small percentage of young men who committed crime or simply behaved badly in public places, then the program would reach all young men.

The youth he wanted to reach often learned from their parents or close relatives how to engage in crime and use violence and drugs. As his center report mentioned, they were "from homes where lawlessness is the norm . . . overt criminal acts, prison sentences, violence and intimidation are quite usual—with the children from an early age being party to such acts and displays of aggression and mindlessness." It is these youth, the report claims, that "by fear and intimidation can influence the rest of the group. All valuable work conducted with the top 98% can be ruined in an instance because of the persuasive control and influence of the final 2%. Until we find credible inroads to this 2%, any (all) social work has the real potential to end in frustration."[15] In other words, these young men had to provide a different sort of example so that others would resist crime.

When I first met the founder in 2004, he brought up the relationship of the center to local government offices almost immediately. He offered the analogy of a new invention rendering obsolete the primary product of a multibillion-dollar company.

> I say what if someone told you that they had invented a car that runs on water? They would make BP [British Petroleum], this multibillion-pound company, very unhappy. You'd next ask them to prove it. To build the car. Well, that is what we have done [in his center]. We've built the car. BP is the government. Just once, I would like a local councilor to come and say "You were right."

To the director, his project theory was far more effective and appropriate for the area in which he worked than the services provided by the local authority. When I first visited the area, the director drove me around to show me the soon-to-be-replaced government community center. It was covered in graffiti, surrounded by barbed-wire fences, and weighted down by surveillance cameras. He recalled that, "When we decided to open the gym, we went to the youth club [run by the local authority] to tell them. Kids set fire to the place while we were there."

In contrast, his building remained free of graffiti and crime. He attributed this apparent respect for the premises to his direct engagement with local business and gang leaders and his involvement of youth in the building process. He also confronted youth early on about damaging or destroying any part of the building.

> When we first came here, some kids threw eggs at the fire exit doors. I found out who it was and went and knocked on their doors. I said, "Is your dad in?" "My dad," the kid answered, "My dad never lived here." "Well, is your mum in?" This kid said she was in the bath. I called up and said, "Your son egged the fire exit." She said, [his name], get your . . . up here. She must have set a record for the number four-letter words in a sentence. What chance does he have? We went to the other kid's house and it was the same thing, "My dad?" like "What?"

The director felt he could make a judgment about family structure because of his trajectory: growing up in the area, belonging to a gang, and eventually marrying, having children, and owning his own business. In other words, he chose the path of social stability and thereby qualified himself to intervene with those likely to make another choice.

For the director, the government officials hired to work on the neighborhood regeneration team belonged to the middle class and thought like the 'middle class,' or educated, professionalized, and self-interested. They commuted to a poor area from their middle-class neighborhoods and thus remained ignorant of all that went on in his ward. They could only offer what they knew but, as he noted, insisted, "You can't provide middle-class solutions for the working class." They also had little personal investment in regeneration. He joked that, "the regeneration committee created the first rush hour [in the area], by all leaving exactly at five." He complained that they rarely chose to live in the area, mentioning several times that even the local Member of Parliament (MP) had elected to live elsewhere. "Why should he [live here]? I don't mean to sound cynical. He earns £60,000–70,000, has kids, a family. Twenty years ago, MPs were genuine representatives of people. I think to be elected MP today is super for the MP."

He was no less cynical and disparaging about staff occupying lower levels of the bureaucratic hierarchy. Describing an incident where he and his team sought materials for building the gym in the nineties, he spoke of government incompetence, lethargy, and disinterest. The local authority had razed ten homes as part of the regeneration effort. Upon learning of this, the center asked to use parts of the now destroyed homes in its own construction project.

> They tore down homes that had been in Wythenshawe for decades, pre-1940. We asked for materials for the gym [then at the beginning stage]. We called and the person would say, "Good idea, you need to call this person . . ." There was one scenario where we actually made a circle; we called one, two, three people and ended up back at the first person. There is this worker who doesn't care, who gets paid minimum wage, and who goes home every day at five and watches TV.

The director used this incident to stress a more general point about the young men and women who frequented his gym or used other services like the mother-toddler club and support for small enterprises. He was also referring to members of the larger population of one of the most deprived wards in England. "People say all the population [of this ward] needs a little support. But these people are survivors. They don't need support. It is the leaders who need support. They need direction. We give them a place of support."[16]

Although his ideas about reaching out to gangs and young criminals attracted media attention and the support of funders like the Church Urban Fund, his disdain for the local bureaucrats provoked mutual antagonism and perhaps isolated the center from the million-pound government projects rising up around it. A member of the local Regeneration Team who had managed funding for the center was very frank in his attitude toward the director. "He [the center founder] thinks I am some middle class guy feeding off the backs of the poor. He once called me a poverty pimp. He was shocked to learn that I live in the area." The employee then added sarcastically, "You know, at his center, he is Top Dog. He is The Man. He pushes that grassroots, man of the people kind of thing. He talks the talk."[17] Personal dislike then, even animosity, overshadowed the exchange of assessments of government projects and the center.

For instance, the church-going director was infuriated that the representative mocked religious belief and the representative suggested the director had little idea or little motivation to learn how to manage an organization transparently and away from informal, perhaps 'unsavory' practices. The representative recounted how he had been invited to a board meeting at a dog racing track ("I didn't attend"). He also had doubts about continuing government funding for the center because of the director's methods in accounting. "There was some confusion about money going to his wife's project at the [center] and the money we gave for another, specific project."

The personal tensions blended with mutual criticisms of the services of the local authority and the center. The Regeneration Team representative considered the founder's class-based criticisms of government action to be ignorant of the process of government management.

> He [the center's founder] thinks we waste millions of pounds on consultants. What he doesn't realize is that we are all run ragged and need people to do this [flips through a five-year plan document]. I agree that sometimes we pay them to tell us what we already know.

What the director did understand about the Regeneration Team was that the government interpreted neighborhood improvement as gentrification and not necessarily direct support for expanding the potential the local community, with its relatively high levels of poverty and low levels of education and training.[18] Investment in projects and support for the inflow of capital through projects like airport expansion were supposed to instigate social change.

The Regeneration Team representative explained to me his vision of social change in a low-income area:

> When I came for an interview, they told me this area was the poorest in the country. I said, "You mean one of the poorest wards." They answered, "No, *the* poorest ward." Well, I have always seen myself as downwardly mobile, so I felt that I finally had arrived.
>
> Now [after several years], I can get an Americano in the area. I feel like when I can get an Americano, my job is done. Parts of the area are no longer

part of the top one percent of deprivation. They are part of the top five or ten percent. Some areas are even out of the top thirty percent. There are pockets where "aspiring to middle class" couples go to live in a leafy area. They used to be able to buy a house for between £40,000–60,000. Now, you can't get anything for under £100,000. They are diluting the population. We now have to upgrade our services to meet demand. We don't want a Poundland [discount store] here. We want a Marks & Spencer. There are couples who don't shop here in the area. They go to John Lewis in Cheadle.

He complained that the skill level of local residents did not match demand, particularly from the nearby airport and other businesses seeking staff. However, revealing again the distance between the project and government officials, a businessman serving on the board of the center contradicted him, hypothesizing that government employers deliberately overlooked them in contracting labor because of their local origins.

The Regeneration Team representative did admit that the center "has gone from being a place where a few people with too much energy went to being a venue. At the beginning, it was acolytes who went there. Now there is a dance studio, the mezzanine, a mother-toddler program." He insisted, though, that, "we have bigger fish to fry [than the center]. We are interested in partnership and mainstreaming." Indeed, in discussing the construction of a government-funded boxing gym in the area, he admitted that he had asked potential gym users if they would want to go a boxing gym at the center instead, if the center succeeded in building one. "Are you going to go to his [the director's] gym or are you going to come to ours?"

An evaluation focusing on the gym or the center alone may collect data on the use of the center's facilities and the criminal records of gym members, perhaps correlated with frequency of using the gym, family structure, education, employment, and income. When I asked the director if he tracked any transformation in the behavior of those youth frequenting the gym that possessed criminal backgrounds, he offered a general, but for an evaluation not adequate, response: "We act as a model. People know our pasts. They see that we come here, we give money to charity." Indeed, other reports on the center (Lynn 2008) have highlighted the same information the director gave me, about activities and influencing through workshops given to other organizations the importance of reaching the 2% of youth engaging in crime and other forms of disruptive public behavior.

It was exactly this interpretation of impact that bothered the Regeneration Team representative, who saw the director as equating the significance of the center's activities with the force of his personality and vision rather than evidence of individual behavioral change. On the other hand, the Regeneration Team appeared to be doing little to counter the director's claim to representing the community, particularly the population the government wanted to influence in order to reduce gang violence and youth crime. As the director told me:

> If you sit here for 4–5 hours, I bet you won't see a single police car drive by. It is not that this is a no-go area. It isn't. People don't have any respect for the police. A police officer can come and tell a couple of kids something, and they will do this [flip them off]. If you need something, you go to the community leader.

Likewise, the antagonism of the Regeneration Team toward the director only enhanced his reputation as a 'man of the people' who 'knew better' than outsider government bureaucrats.

The consequences of personal antagonism and more profound patterns of social differentiation between local residents and policymakers were that the project remained tightly under the control of the director, and the local government remained distant from the groups it needed to reach as part of its effort to generate social change. The breakdown restricted the development of the service, the organization, and its impact and essentially facilitated the reproduction of the interventions designed to support young people at risk. The next chapter returns to the question of reproduction and how it can be disrupted.

Analyzing Opportunities for Increasing Service and Organizational Effectiveness

Several prominent and widely used evaluation, management, and social research methods focus primarily on how to utilize internal resources to innovate and adapt when faced with environmental pressures, crises, and change. These models stress adopting a constructive and positive approach, rather than concentrating on more negative problem-solving. For instance, what resources do organizations have that can help overcome a threat, such as declining funding or difficulties with a particular program? How should social programs transform to address shifting characteristics of their service user population, different policy directions and access to resources, and/or varied success with specific activities?

One approach, 'resilience,' highlights individual and collective capacity to overcome challenging life circumstances and external disasters. The Resilience Research Centre defines resilience as the capacity, when faced with adversity for "individuals to navigate their way to the psychological, social, cultural, and physical resources that sustain their well-being." Collectively and individually, these resources should "be provided in culturally meaningful ways."[19] Everly specifically associates organizational resilience with 'resilient leadership,' which he defines as the ability to demonstrate "four core attributes of optimism, decisiveness, integrity, and open communications." Leaders who possess these qualities inspire their staff, building the appropriate organizational culture to respond effectively to challenging conditions, whether through innovating services or investing in staff morale and well-being (Everly 2011).[20]

A similar management model, used as well in social science research (e.g. Liebling et al. 1999; Liebling 2015), which focuses on developing positive aspects of an existing service or organization is Appreciative Inquiry (AI). Founded by David Cooperrider, a professor at Case Western University in the United States, AI assumes that organizations are socially constructed rather than objective facts. From this assumption, anything is possible. As Gervase Bushe writes, AI is:

> a method for studying and changing social systems (groups, organizations, communities) that advocates collective inquiry into the best of what is in order to imagine what could be, followed by collective design of a desired future state that is compelling and thus, does not require the use of incentives, coercion or persuasion for planned change to occur.
>
> (2013: 1)

Moreover, "The AI model seeks to create processes of inquiry that will result in better, more effective, convivial, sustainable and vital social systems. It assumes this requires widespread engagement by those who will ultimately implement change" (1).

In evaluation, the parallel method is Developmental Evaluation, founded by Michael Quincy Patton. In an early article (1994), he writes:

> From a developmental perspective, you do something different because something has changed-your understanding, the characteristics of participants, technology, or the world. Those changes are dictated by your current perceptions, but the commitment to change doesn't carry a judgment that what was done before was inadequate or less effective. Change is not necessarily progress. Change is adaptation.
>
> (313)

Patton cites a program director, who said, "we did the best we knew how with what we knew and the resources we had. Now we're at a different place in our development-doing and thinking different things. That's development. That's change. But it's not necessarily improvement" (313). The method itself prioritizes flexibility, responsiveness to change, learning through experience and analysis of external and internal conditions, and working without fixed, often imposed, deadlines, if possible. The evaluator ideally works from within the organization, rather than as an external consultant preparing a report, often to a funder, assessing process and impact within a particular time period. Patton describes the evaluator as "often part of a development team whose members collaborate to conceptualize, design, and test new approaches in a long-term, ongoing process of continuous development, adaptation, and experimentation, keenly sensitive to unintended results and side effects" (Patton 2010: 1). In sum, the role of evaluation and those who do it must account for expected or unexpected transformation, or even minor alterations, in the context in which an organization works, its own operations, and individual service user needs and characteristics, differentiating Developmental Evaluation from standard approaches (Gamble 2008).

Gamble distinguishes the innovation incorporated into Developmental Evaluation from 'improvement,' because it "causes reorganization at a systems level and can occur at the level of an organization, a network or society at large" (15). This reorganization still depends, however, on the internal effort of an organization and the analysis of how its services must adjust to shifting circumstances. As with determining the effect of external constraints on categorization of the social problem and impact and organizational capacity, the systematic analysis of opportunities in the context and how they are translated into assets across and by individual organizations should reveal how external conditions influence conceptions of the problem, interventions, and indicators of positive individual and collective impact and organizational development. This analysis entails, as it did with examining constraints, understanding the political economy of social action. In other words, the analysis should separate out external factors–like institutional behavior, competition for resources and resource management, and local and national politics–from internal factors like decision-making, staff morale, and performance, and ultimately, the ability to affect change at an organizational and individual level.

For instance, external factors can affect trust between staff and beneficiaries, and sometimes their families, influencing quality of service and its impact. Analyzing trust and cooperatives, Hatak et al. (2016) refer to maxim-based trust, which "involves a broader array of resource exchange including socio- emotional support. Repeated interactions create expanded resources, including shared information, status, and concern (1228). In a study of community nurses working in Ceara, Brazil, Tendler and Freedheim stressed the importance of trust to the success of the program:

> When agents talked about why they liked their jobs, the subject of respect from clients and from "my community" often dominated their conversation—much more, interestingly, than the subject of respect from supervisors or other superiors. The trust that was central to the workings of the health program was inspired by quite mundane activities . . . "She is a true friend," a mother said of the health agent working in her community. "She's done more for us than she'll ever realize."
>
> (1994: 1784)

The trust between clients and the larger community was so significant in inspiring quality performance that it was hard to differentiate its effects from external performance monitoring (1785).

Likewise, frontline workers I have interviewed have consistently argued against micro-managing a service, such as allotting specific time limits for home visits, because this approach does not allow necessary relationships to develop that make services effective. In interviews conducted in 2009 in Sheffield, both the director of a carers center and of a church-based support service for older people were critical both of the government's dismissal of low-level demands of carers, namely housecleaning, and the provision of related services by large organizations, which adopted managerial models of delivery. The director of the carers center said that, "people who have really low-level needs are being pushed back, like those who want shopping or cleaning windows." She added, "I overheard an assistant director say 'Older people don't die from say, not having their windows cleaned or not having a bath.' You know, quite hard-nosed about it."[21] In other words, faced with scarce resources–urgent needs, for instance–support at home after a hospital discharge became the priority.

When large organizations like Age Concern[22] did provide support for low-level tasks, both directors felt the work was too standardized, or devoid of feeling.[23] The director of the carers center noted that Age Concern was "increasing 'little chunks of tasks' like five minutes for a microwaveable meal, but there's no social interaction in it." The director of the church-based program complained that though Age Concern offered a carpentry service, she could never reach them. She said:

> They have paperwork and the things they have to do. I don't even call them anymore for handyman services. They are chock-a-block full with two services they should focus on—homecare and handymen. I call Stayput [a local organization specializing in handyman services] who sends someone out immediately.

Though she did not mention the opportunity to develop a personal relationship and subsequent trust explicitly, it was evident in the distance she conveyed from the managerial approach of Age Concern.

She was also uncertain large organizations could become intensively engaged with a community, given its size and mission as the chapter of a national organization.

> I am here. I am in the community. And I am touching just the tip of the iceberg. People who are older sometimes don't want to admit they need something, that they are lonely. But they don't need to have a problem to use our service. They just have to be older.

The other director, of the church-based support service, stressed that her volunteer and paid staff

> pay attention to people, we listen to people. We also get phenomenally positive feedback from our service users. . . . It is about human nature, being

kind, being caring. People come out needing only small amounts of help so you can feel like you have made a difference. They don't get that from Social Services.

She offered as an example a story of a man she visited over the course of three to four months (eight or nine visits) who had lost his wife. After this period, she introduced him to a lunch club where he made friends.

Until you've sorted the care out, you can't let go of them. I see people at the clubs. I always meet up with the organizers and ask if there is anyone giving them concern. I might go visit and tell them to give me a call.

For her, though she could not serve the same number of older people as a larger organization, her intensive care revealed the needs of individuals rather than problems and needs elaborated by policymakers and likewise, indicated necessary interventions.

Another organization in Sheffield working with older people showed how opportunities to access material and social resources, institutional contacts, and political support can together be translated into assets to enhance effectiveness and sustainability. This organization, where I conducted research in 2006, assists older people suffering from dementia by providing a 'day out' to individuals with dementia and still living at home. At the time, the organization employed a full-time nurse and a part-time administrator. The nurse was on loan from the Sheffield Health and Social Care Trust and the City Council paid for the administrator and the locale of the organization, or a church hall.

The nurse arrived in the late nineties when the organization's board of trustees decided to change their approach to dementia care and requested that the NHS send a nurse to advise them. The service at that time was institutionally oriented rather than 'person-centered.' In the institutional model, staff led on activities and the service users watched them. The person-centered approach to dementia care, developed by Tom Kitwood and the Bradford Dementia Group at the University of Bradford (Kitwood 1993, 1997; Mitchell and Agnelli 2015) encourages the abilities that still exist among patients. They participate in arts and crafts, games, reading, and cleaning up. In addition, the staff, including student nurses interning with the program and volunteers, eat with the service users and engage them in conversation.

The organization and the service were able to thrive, despite assisting small numbers of beneficiaries and reliance on annual renewal of government funding, and thus continued political interest in dementia, because the lead was seconded, or on loan, from the public sector. Her job situation created an overlap between the charity and the public health service, allowing for better flow of information and management of patient care. The nurse reported her work to her supervisor, ensuring public sector awareness of the organization and regular communication about individual patients. The nurse also knew how to maneuver linguistically and behaviorally within a public sector agency plagued by financial and management problems. Her knowledge of the discourse and objectives of budget planners meant that the nurse could categorize the approach of the service as slowing a progressive disease and present its delivery as inexpensive, high value, and ultimately low risk.

At the same time, her autonomy allowed her to develop a service based on intensive care and avoid too much emphasis on numeric targets. The nurse noted that, "Because I am working in the voluntary sector, my line managers have trouble managing me. For example, if I ask about developing an outreach measure, they say 'Does it cost anything?' 'No.' 'Then do what you think is best.'" She added, "Because [the organization] is seen as a beacon of good practice, we very rarely receive criticism [from the NHS]. I also don't represent a problem to them." This lack of criticism was due to the absence of any visible problems or difficulties. She said, "Everything in the Trust [local authority of the NHS] is balanced on risk. And I am seen as low-risk. Because we supervise them [service users] closely and we are all in the same room. I am not going to them with problems."[24] The service thus offered benefits without evident or potential downsides, enabling her supervisor and other managers to approve its continuation without spending time investigating the merit of this continuation.

The confidence in the program's overall quality allowed for more attentive individual care, which in turn, prevented institutionalization or admission into permanent care. This care is paid for by the state and typically not reversible. More specifically, she could keep individuals listed as service users to see if they improved while still at home. She could also discuss the individual's health problems with the relevant Social Services and NHS staff and avoid criticism for not increasing numbers of service users (value for money). The nurse explained:

> We can be very flexible with our services. We have quite a lot of autonomy. For example, we have a chap who has just broken his femur. He is in the hospital now and if we were in Social Services, we would have discharged him [from their list]. But because we are here, we have not discharged him.

She could then wait for him to come home and restart his participation in the program, offering him the chance to stay in his own house longer. She cited a service user who had suffered a heart attack and a stroke.

> I went to see his wife and told her we would save his place though he was in hospital for three months. We left a green light for him. We could tell Social Services what we did. They didn't tell us what to do, even though they thought we could have used the place during the three months. He came back at 86 for two times and then died. His case left them [other service users] with the hope that they can go home from the hospital.

These two examples indicate the benefit of blurred boundaries between sectors, and more broadly, how the opportunity presented by the overlap can be transformed into an asset for the organization and its service. For this organization, regular communication with the local health service allowed it to provide a better end of life experience for service users and save the expense of publicly funded full-time care.

This communication, as well as committed, long-term volunteers, involvement of both local universities, particularly regarding student placement, and political support enabled the organization to survive in an increasingly difficult economic climate (at the time of publication, its services are being put out to tender by the city council). The nurse did lament at the time of the research that "The government needs to put more money in the beginning as prevention. For example, by not helping those who are low-risk, everyone ends up high-risk." The nurse insisted that

> We have people who, if we'd pulled out, would be in permanent care. And the carers couldn't cope. We provide a respite.... If you are a carer and you

are looking after your husband, and you get to a breaking point and you call Social Services, Social Services intervene and there is no way back. It is very rare to get out of permanent care.

She was despairing about general funds available for dementia. In 2006, she told me:

> Services for older people are generally pretty poor. Services for mental health, whether you are young or old, are poor. If you are old and have dementia, you are below the system. . . . In funding terms, people with dementia are way down the line. If you are fundraising, if you have a baby hooked up to a machine and you have an older person with dementia sitting in a corner who is probably incontinent, it is not very attractive.

The comparative funding situation, at least for research and innovative practice, has not, unfortunately, changed significantly over the past decade relative to costs to health and social services in the United Kingdom. According to Luengo-Fernandez et al. (2015), dementia care cost an estimated £11.6 billion compared with £5 billion for cancer, £2.9 billion for stroke, and £2.5 billion for coronary heart disease (CHD). The Alzheimer's Society has estimated a total cost of £23 billion, including the equivalent cost of family carers (2015). Yet, for every £10 of costs, £1.08 in research funding went to cancer, £0.65 to CHD, £0.19 to stroke, and £0.08 to dementia (2015). The government did pledge £150 million to establish a Dementia Research Institute, to be opened by 2020.[25]

Conclusion: Why Think in Terms of a Field?

The financial picture for dementia research and the costs of care and the perceived distance in 2016 between political and policymaking elites and individual citizens, particularly in areas suffering from decades of underinvestment and deprivation like that of the gym, represent important environmental conditions for new and existing projects in dementia care and at-risk youth support. The combination of constraints and opportunities affect not only the relationship between one organizations and services across an area of work and thus the analysis should, in principle, extend to examining patterns within the area regarding conceptualization of problems and needs, types of interventions, organizational characteristics, and impact indicators.

The next chapter develops a framework for analyzing how areas of social intervention, or fields of social action, become constituted and are reproduced, influencing the kinds of services and organizations that develop and survive and their effect on social change. The chapter also suggests how to alter fields by accounting for the connection between range of factors in service and organizational effectiveness, such as staff motivation; social relations between staff and service users, and the expression of trust; communication between the public and voluntary or nonprofit sectors; understanding of need and impact; funding sources; and social networks. Some of these factors do not appear in evaluation models that focus on tangible inputs into measurable results (like number of youth accompanied when interviewed or detained at the police station), but are significant in service delivery and instigating individual behavioral and attitudinal change.

Notes

1 Interview with volunteer, February 15, 2009.

2 Barnardos was established in 1867 by Dr. Thomas Barnardo, who founded a school to help children living and working on the streets of London. Today, the organization engages in adoption and foster care services, research policy and consultation, and counseling on issues like domestic violence. The organization runs almost 400 projects in the United Kingdom and manages stores that support the organization financially.

3 Sova was founded in 1975 by volunteers working with the Inner London Probation Service. The now national organization focuses primarily on reducing crime among vulnerable communities, particularly youth, through pairing volunteer mentors with individuals leaving or connected to the penal system to provide emotional support and even teaching of basic skills, like reading and writing.

4 Specifically, the report cited the following as "important for moving away from offending" (2016: 7): "a balanced, trusting and consistent working relationship with at least one worker . . . meaningful personal relationships and a sense of belonging to family, emotional support, practical help and where the worker clearly believed in the capacity of the child or young person to desist from offending, the development of a strong relationship and/or becoming a parent, changing peer and friendship groups, interventions which provided problem solving solutions to use in day-to-day life situations,[and] well planned and relevant restorative justice interventions" (7–8).

5 In fact, the same organization still runs the project.

6 www.mentoring.org/program_resources/elements_and_toolkits

7 Citizens Advice Bureau describes itself as the following: "The Citizens Advice service helps people to resolve their problems. As the UK's largest advice provider we are equipped to deal with any issue, from anyone, spanning debt and employment to consumer and housing plus everything in between. In the last year alone, the Citizens Advice service helped 2.1 million people with 6.6 million problems. But we're not just here in times of crisis – we also use clients' stories anonymously to campaign for policy changes that benefit the population as a whole. (Citizens Advice Introduction to the Service 2012-13, p. 1)."

8 Interview with staff member, October 25, 2006.

9 Investopedia defines 'bottleneck' as "A point of congestion in a system that occurs when workloads arrive at a given point more quickly than that point can handle them. The inefficiencies brought about by the **bottleneck** often create a queue and a longer overall cycle time." www.investopedia.com/terms/b/bottleneck.asp

10 The assumption of transferability has also frequently been criticized. For instance, critiquing project design in international development, Martin Ravallion calls for acknowledging heterogeneity among local institutional and economic contexts, participant characteristics, and impacts when implementing a project in multiple locations (2008).

11 Interview with director, May 16, 2008.

12 Funded by the Nuffield Foundation.

13 www.independent.co.uk/news/uk/politics/dwp-fit-to-work-esa-appeal-tribunal-a6923066.html

14 www.theguardian.com/society/2016/jan/27/the-bedroom-tax-explained

15 Interview with director, October 13, 2004.

16 A colleague at the small, faith-based charity where I worked in Washington, DC made a similar comment about drug users. "They are the most entrepreneurial people around, real survivors," she said. "They go out every day and get the money they need to get drugs." I believe she was not referring primarily to crime, with the exception of prostitution, but rather to whatever petty job or source of money the individual could access to make it through a daily habit.

17 Interview with government official, October 28, 2004.

18 Among the key objectives for the Wythenshawe Strategic Regeneration Framework, adopted in 2004, are promoting housing investment, seeking job opportunities through the expansion of Manchester Airport, improving shopping facilities, making the area attractive to investors, widening the spectrum of job opportunities, increasing the physical appeal of the area through landscaping, supporting cultural activities, improving transport, and improving self-identity. Education and health services were also listed. The point is not to deny the importance of these objectives but to demonstrate how they differed from the vision of the director, who claimed to know better what local residents wanted. *Wythenshawe Strategic Regeneration Framework*, December 2004, p. 3, http://www.manchester.gov.uk/info/500110/wythenshawe_regeneration/2422/wythenshawe_strategic_regeneration_framework

19 http://resilienceresearch.org
20 https://hbr.org/2011/06/building-a-resilient-organizat
21 Interview with director, May 16, 2007.
22 Age Concern is the United Kingdom's largest charitable organization working with older people. It was founded during World War II and now operates all over the United Kingdom, running Age Concern charity shops and social services, from home visiting to housing assistance.
23 On a larger scale, a survey of carers conducted for Sheffield Carers Centre found that the services respondents wanted more of were home visits, a drop-in service, longer telephone hours and a bereavement service; in other words, services requiring empathy, proximity, availability, and flexibility. Published in the February 2009 newsletter of the Sheffield Carers Centre, p. 8.
24 Interview with nurse, April 17, 2007.
25 www.gov.uk/guidance/appropriate-adults-guide-for-youth-justice-professionals

CHAPTER 3

ANALYZING FIELDS OF SOCIAL ACTION

The Appropriate Adult Scheme in England and Wales, because of its straightforward design, demonstrates the conceptual boundaries and limitations on social intervention generated by a field. Mandated by law in 1984, the Appropriate Adult Scheme addresses one problem, provides one solution across different providers, and is assessed through one criterion. The basic assumption underlying the Appropriate Adult Scheme is that young people or vulnerable adults require assistance during detention to prevent abuse. Historically, the Scheme originated in England with the Police and Criminal Evidence Act of 1984 (PACE). The law responded to reports in the sixties and seventies of police eliciting false confessions from vulnerable suspects (Pritchard 2007). PACE mandated that all people age 17 and younger, and those older than 17 with mental health problems and learning difficulties, required an appropriate adult present when questioned by the police.[1] After the passage of PACE, Social Services and voluntary sector organizations put together teams of paid workers, volunteers, or a combination of both.

The service has since been affected by time restrictions on youth custody, which have translated into a limited timeframe for Appropriate Adults to arrive at police stations. After the initial mandate was passed, if the police could not contact the parents, a social worker, or a designated Appropriate Adult, then they would have to keep the young person in detention for hours. Youth could spend longer in custody than detainees without this requirement. In their frustration, the police would occasionally drop cases. In response, the Crime and Disorder Act of 1998 required local authorities in partnership with other relevant statutory bodies, namely the Police and Probation Service, to establish Youth Offending Teams. These Teams were given the explicit responsibility to ensure that adults were present during questioning to "safeguard the interests of children and young persons detained or questions by police officers."[2] In 2004, the Youth Justice Board recommended a maximum two-hour wait for Appropriate Adult Services.[3]

When the service is contracted out to charities or companies, rather than Social Services, it cannot be altered or integrated into a consortium of youth-oriented interventions. Mandated through law and government oversight, the narrow substance of the field of social action has, in turn, influenced its structure. Although at least one organization (The Appropriate Adult Service) is national, the majority of organizations are local and bid to manage the Scheme in the particular area.[4] The requirements of the Scheme mean that only organizations with sufficient capacity to recruit and manage enough volunteers or staff[5] and to respond to police call-outs can realistically compete for the contract.[6]

This transparent and simple structure has implications at a collective level for organizations that work with youth and at an individual organizational level. On a collective level, because Youth Offending Teams contract out the Scheme out to one agency in each area, the field generates competitiveness at the bidding stage. Furthermore, though voluntary sector organizations providing a number of youth-oriented services typically run the Appropriate Adult Schemes, they do not link them explicitly or even informally with their other services, despite overlapping target populations.[7] Any action taken in addition to advocacy during detention can only occur on an ad hoc basis. At an organizational level, executives and managers may regard the Scheme, as the Sova volunteer noted, as a funding possibility and an addition to overall mission and external identity but not as part of a more general effort to confront the causes of youth offending.[8] In other words, the narrow logic of intervention means that the service exists apart from a larger debate about the availability and quality of public and voluntary sector services for youth offenders.[9]

On a practical level, Service Level Agreements measure effectiveness by response to police call-outs, which means that project managers have to prioritize recruiting a sufficient number of volunteers who are readily accessible and available. In Sheffield, a university town, this may mean students with flexible schedules and typically no family obligations. In fact, the project manager told me that training for the Scheme had to teach volunteers how to act as a responsible adult with young people who had been detained. Most were men often barely younger than volunteers, who, at the time, were generally female. The importance of recruitment may in turn prevent allocating the time necessary for other aspects of the project, for instance, communication between volunteers and project managers. The long-term volunteer at Sova complained that the overstretched managers had little time to build 'esprit de corps' among the volunteers and paid staff and little time to discuss personally volunteer input into the quality of the service. The volunteer claimed he knew few, if any, of the other volunteers and he never showed up for volunteer meetings.

Lastly, the Schemes are typically underfunded. According to a 2006 report (Pritchard: 8), or years before austerity measures introduced in 2010, by the National Network of Appropriate Adults, the median level of funding at the time—£43,500—was generally about half of what is voluntary sector organizations appeared to need to manage an effective service operating all year from 8 a.m. to midnight. NAAN estimated the correct amount at £90,000.[10] In a 2015 report on Appropriate Adult (AA) services for mentally vulnerable adults, conducted for the Home Office, the Network found that the "annual cost of ensuring full provision of trained AAs from organised schemes, throughout the custody process and across England and Wales, is estimated at £19.5 million (£113,000 per local authority)" (Bath et al. 2015: 2). However, national spending was estimated "to be in excess of £3 million per year" (2).

Addressing the ambitions of social interventions and problems like resources, this chapter outlines an approach to analyzing and altering fields of social action that combines practical questions with exploring existing research and conducting new action research. The aim of analyzing existing fields is to understand how they are constituted and reproduce themselves, and the implications for both categorizing and addressing specific social problems and encouraging or circumscribing broader trajectories of social change. This analysis should, in turn, facilitate developing alternative ideas of intervention that may include new conceptions of social issues and problems and expectations of social and individual impact.

More specifically, the chapter brings together my own ethnographic research on social action, social theory, research on organizational behavior, and evaluation research and practical models to show fields of social action can be analyzed. As demonstrated ahead, fields can be delineated through the connections they generate between conceptions of social problems, types of intervention, and desired impact, and organizational characteristics and decision-making. The analysis explores the relative influence of contextual factors, for example, policy, on the constitution and reproduction of the field, and likewise suggests necessary transformation in the context to alter the field. In developing a conceptual framework for analyzing fields of social action, the aim is to make their constitution and reproduction a self-conscious effort from within.

Analyzing a Field

The conceptual framework proposed here suggests understanding the design and impact of social projects through analyzing the political economy of social action and, likewise, improving design and impact through challenging the ideology, politics, distribution of resources, and institutional behavior that perpetuate a particular area of social action.

The framework connects policy and practice at three points. The first is epistemological, making knowledge and communication, and thus social relations, within social action the basis for developing conceptual frameworks of social change and thus for influencing health and social policy. The second, to look across a field of work, is both analytic and methodological. Organization business plans, project evaluations, whether qualitative or quantitative, and assessments of organizational capacity generally focus on single organizations and the impact of its services or coordination between organizations. Some tools, like network analysis (Davies 2009), which are used by aid agencies and domestic organizations alike, mention the relations that organizations have with service users and other stakeholders like funding agencies but they still ultimately stress changing the organization to generate greater impact in its services. The third point of contact is practical. Relating the design and impact of specific projects to the context means acknowledging and processing information about how services work that is often obscured or marginalized in reports about frontline delivery and project management. For instance, qualitative data about the interpretations of nonprofit organization employees and local public officials of social problems and, on a more emotive level, demonstrations of trust and respect between service users and staff or between staff and managers now become part of the analysis of a field and project evaluation.

The following section illustrates how to analyze a field by asking three sets of questions aimed at understanding (1) the basis of the field, or how conceptions of social problems correspond with organizational characteristics; (2) how external forces influence the reproduction of a field; and (3) the resistance encountered by efforts to transform a field. The first question asks if there is a prevalent interpretation of the social problem and a prevalent service design. Which external factors influence particular interpretation of a social problem and related service design— is it policy, institutional behavior, access to resources, social mobilization around the issue, or a combination of some or all of these factors? Are there similar characteristics between organizations that share the same conception of the problem and offer similar services? Are less common services associated with smaller, community-based organizations? This analysis should indicate if there is a relationship between delivering a particular service and organizational characteristics and sustainability, contributing to the reproduction of the field.

Another set of questions concerns discrepancies and agreement between organizations and policymakers regarding the conception of the problem. More pointedly, what are the implications of concordance and friction between organizations, public institutions, private funding bodies, and policymakers for addressing need, demonstrating impact, developing services, and ultimately, sustaining the field? Which services survive and which services and organizations decline? Responding to these questions can show how fields themselves survive through shifting patterns of dominance and marginality between services and organizations. The third set of questions asks why organizations alter their interpretation of a social problem and adjust their service accordingly. Can organizations cope with a transformation in their mission and services and if not, why not? The response to these questions can reveal the factors that circumscribe potential transformation of a field, and inversely, the expectations of service impact that perpetuate a field.

Determining the Possibility of a 'Field'

As a conceptual framework, a field of social action draws upon a substantial body of research that has examined the influence of the context on organizational characteristics and behavior. The question often tested in this literature (see Dimaggio and Powell 1983, 1991; Meyer and Rowan 1977; Zucker

1987) is if factors like regulation and ambiguous goals produce isomorphism, or homogeneity, among nonprofit organizations, especially in the same area of work. As Dimaggio and Powell (1983) write in what has become the foundational article in this literature, "We seek to explain homogeneity, not variation. In the initial stages of their life cycle, organizational fields display considerable diversity in approach and form. Once a field becomes well established, however, there is an inexorable push towards homogenization" (148). Coercive, mimetic, and normative isomorphism produce institutional isomorphism. Coercive isomorphism relates to legitimizing norms established through policy and politics; mimetic isomorphism from regularized responses to uncertainty; and normative isomorphism, from the pressure to professionalize (150). The neo-institutional approach their work has inspired, along with that of other scholars like Meyer and Rowan (1977), contends that external pressure to present business-like management structures and report certain outputs to justify service value and thus funding can affect how organizations are run, or their structure and mission. The assumption is that nonprofits, as Alexander writes (2000), "will conform to norms asserted by the dominant actors" (290).

However, a number of studies (Leiter 2005; Roy et al. 2015; Claeyé and Jackson 2012) dispute this assumption. Scholars have instead argued that their dependence on environmental factors like local politics and internal factors like values and leadership (Ramanath 2009; Steane and Christie 2001; Cadena-Roa et al. 2011) to achieve goals and inherent connection in their activities to the nature of the social problems they are trying to address (Oliver 1991), prevents this push toward isomorphism. Roy et al. claim that neo-institutionalism is "problematic since the employment of business development as a means to overcome poverty or social exclusion requires an understanding of the specific socio-economic environment in which that development is to take place" (2015: 2538). They write, "[T]o be 'effective' means engaging in an ongoing process of evaluating the impact of the organization upon the community through questioning, verifying and redefining the manner of interaction with the environment" (2015: 2538). Indeed, Leiter expresses relief that significant isomorphism has not characterized the sector:

> To close on a more prescriptive note, we should likely be relieved that the nonprofit sector is not characterized by substantial isomorphism. Many of the sector's greatest values depend on variety, not similarity: responsiveness

to minority needs and preferences, resistance to corporate and bureaucratic hegemony, and availability as a social laboratory all require variety, not isomorphism.

(2013: 1067)

Aligica goes further than analyzing diversity in organizational forms by exploring decision-making and behavior in cooperation. Drawing on Hayek's work, Aligica emphasizes the role of 'discovery, imagination, and creativity' (2015: 1036) in cooperation. He writes,

> The key assumption of the "symbiotics" perspective and its model is that individuals have a rich set of endowments and skills and engage in voluntary cooperation in which they share their capacities (through transactions or association). Thus, they create a large variety of cooperative formulae and institutional arrangements.

(2015: 1036)

Individuals searching voluntarily for solutions to common problems may arrive at complex arrangements that involve different sets of rules and procedures for collective enforcement of the rules. In other words, the process of micro-level decision-making and behavior is not easily discernible or, more specifically, based on utilitarian logic.

Despite agreement on the diversity of organizational forms and modes and processes of cooperation among nonprofits, other research points to identifiable patterns of organizational survival. In their research on the impact of welfare reform in the United States in the nineties on social service organizations, Reisch and Sommerfeld (2003) note that competitive funding environments can put smaller organizations at a disadvantage, as they lack the internal capacity, or staff and appropriate software, to find new funding resources. Though some research, as noted earlier, points to diversity in social relations as preventing isomorphism, other research points to characteristics of social networks that support the survival of young organizations. Pedrini et al. (2016) offer guidance to new organizations on the kinds of networks to build:

> [I]n order to create a solid and effective organisation, initial partners—founders and members—should be limited in number and chosen with care in order to create a team of people who already know one another or at

least within which there are groups of people who already have ties. At the same time, the team should not be self-reliant and self- inclusive, but rather the involved founders and members should have relationships outside the organisation, which may be facilitated by choosing members from different contexts which, nonetheless, must be close enough to share a common vision.

(2016: 1212)

Reisch and Sommerfeld (2003) suggest that access to appropriate networks is linked to how organizations present themselves, particularly those involving government officials and others in control of funding provisions. If smaller, though not necessarily younger, organizations cannot follow legitimizing norms, namely adoption of business methods of management and fundraising, then they will struggle to become appealing to funding bodies. For some organizations, especially those rooted in their communities or faith, with a mission to serve the most vulnerable, the pressure to change as an organization conflicts with their ethos (Reisch and Sommerfeld 2003; Alexander 2000).

Considering fields of social action as a conceptual framework entails developing Reisch and Sommerfeld's association of organizational size and resources, including social networks, with interpretations of the social problem and related interventions. In their analysis of homeless shelters (2005), Emirbeyer and Williams offer a useful schema for relating services to organizational characteristics. While they do not make the leap to assessing the impact of a service, they offer an example of how organizations and services can come to dominate the structure of a field. In their analysis, they distinguish between types of shelters and predict their status within the Department of Homeless Services according to their social capital. Two types of shelters dominate the field: those that maintain order through regulating clients' actions and processing housing placements smoothly, and those that possess few resources and accept clients struggling with drug abuse and/or mental health issues. Their position of dominance in the field reflects the two politically and socially valued attributes of shelters, or order and authenticity. The first enforces rules in order to evidence individual behavioral change and functionality within the housing system, and the second gains "legitimacy from being the real deal, from working with the most disadvantaged clients. These are the shelters that can point to being on the front lines or in the trenches, fighting the good fight against homelessness" (2005: 700).

Those shelters lacking either form of capital occupy the 'dominated regions' of the field, which may translate, according to Emirbeyer and Williams, into fewer resources, high turnover among staff and likewise, low morale, and the assignment of clients the Department of Homeless Services found the most intransigent and difficult. Emirbeyer and Williams note that

> Homeless clients who are identified by the DHS as chronic, long-term stayers, especially those with aggressive dispositions and less social capital, tend to remain in the less privileged shelters. By contrast, temporarily homeless people, those who typically bear larger amounts of capital of various kinds, make the move rather quickly into more privileged settings.
>
> (2005: 703)

The state, predictably, concentrates its efforts on the least problematic service users because through service users moving to more permanent residences, government officials can demonstrate impact and success.

In turn, the need for state approval, or social capital, can dilute or reshape organizational aims. Dimaggio and Powell (1983) argue that ambiguity in substantive mission produces isomorphism, claiming, "[O]rganizations with ambiguous or disputed goals are likely to be highly dependent upon appearances for legitimacy. Such organizations may find it to their advantage to meet the expectations of important constituencies about how they should be designed and run." They add, "We contend that, in most situations, reliance on established, legitimated procedures enhances organizational legitimacy and survival characteristics" (155).

Questioning the Conception of the Social Problem

However, what happens when the goals are unambiguous because the social problem and intervention are well defined and clearly designed? The absence of ambiguity in substantive goals may generate cohesion across diverse organizational forms, whereas ambivalence about the identified social problem and the effectiveness of existing interventions can disrupt this cohesion. What factors influence maintaining a particular conception of a social problem and related intervention across diverse organizations? Which factors compel organizations to alter their concept and related services?

The neo-institutional approach correlates homogenizing forces in the environment, such as external regulation or predominance of particular educational and social backgrounds among board members (Abzug and Galaskiewicz 2001; Hwang and Powell 2009), with increasingly homogenous patterns in decision-making. Critics of this approach contend that internal diversity prevents predicting decision-making processes. Comparing how three NGOs in India interact with the government in Mumbai, Ramanath (2009) shows that human and material resources and the founding values and local expectations of the organization can cause different responses to external pressures. He comments that:

> Path-dependent processes make it difficult for organizations to explore alternative options. New forms and ways of doing things do arise but are typically described as processes wrought with constraints—a major one being the embeddedness of the organization in its founding conditions (including founding values, technologies, knowledge, and other supporting structures and resources).
>
> (2009: 67)

Yet, at the same time, local and national environmental factors like trends in economic growth and the job market, political interest in the particular social issue and expectations of the role of charities in addressing it, and institutional behavior can predict consistency in how a problem is conceptualized, and likewise prevent or hinder the emergence of alternatives. Job placement services for low-income, low-skill men and women, typically reliant on public benefits and sometimes with a criminal record, can offer an example of both consistency and the challenge of offering a different kind of service. These services typically focus on job placement—or providing support for writing a CV, preparing for an interview, and looking for a job. They may aim for long-term job retention and social mobility, as well as, inversely, not returning to destructive behavior like crime or drug addiction. Some of the larger organizations, like Goodwill and the Center for Employment Opportunities (CEO) in the United States, provide transitional employment, for instance, in

Goodwill retail stores, in order for individuals to experience the regularity and demands of paid employment. The emphasis in the service is entirely on cultivating individual behavioral patterns like patience, discipline, and reliability. The CEO brochure describes its transitional work sites as teaching "the behaviors that employers say they value the most."[11] These consist of "showing up on time, taking direction from a supervisor, working hard, being good co-workers and showing good communication skills" (2009: 67). The work sites are managed by a CEO employee, who pays the participants by check at the end of each full-day shift.

The impact that organizations note on their websites likewise concerns individual job retention and mobility and corresponding positive changes in self-image. Advertising a 'head, hands, heart' approach, the job placement service at Pecan, a small London-based organization, explains how helping individuals in a vulnerable position, whether because of a criminal record or simply long periods of unemployment, to become more self-confident can assist in turn with finding a job. The approach "teaches the three pieces of information job seekers should tell their potential employers; the head knowledge they have (such as qualifications), the hands-on experience they have gained and the heart they have for that particular job."[12] A case study from the Goodwill website demonstrates how mentoring support and the experience of finding and retaining a job can generate dramatic changes in self-identity. A man who had attended a work opportunities session at Goodwill after 15 years in prison emphasized how his life had changed through work:

> I came to Goodwill a drastically different person then I am today. I was unsure of myself, lacking self confidence and very afraid. I had an extensive history of failures, of broken promises and many setbacks. Today I am no longer any of those things—I am confident, self-aware, capable, and most of all, overcome with hope that the future I once feared, is now filled with promise and the fruit of all I have worked to achieve.[13]

The stress on individual transformation before and after job placement is consistent across organizations and services. At the same time, there is little advocacy for better conditions regarding low-wage, low-skill jobs, which may in turn improve retention rates and continued self-belief and positive motivation. Most charities, facing limited, often unpredictable, resources, do not have this capacity or may fear alienating their dependable employers, whom they are already asking to hire at-risk individuals.

Yet, while the 'problem' and 'impact' continue to center on overcoming personal histories, or without comparable attention to the local labor market, the ability to instigate more widespread social change among particularly marginalized populations remains constrained. Two job placement projects, one in Washington, DC, and one in Manchester, United Kingdom, demonstrate both the challenge of going beyond an applicant-centered service and the link between the accepted identification of the problem, service design, and organizational characteristics, management, and sustainability. In analyzing the link, rather than reveal how internal and external factors influence organizational diversity, the comparison shows how these factors support the perpetuation of a particular theory of change and categorization of social impact across organizations, regardless of size, and likewise, the stability of the field. The 'problem' addressed by organizations and likewise in the Theory of Change, is unemployment and its negative repercussions, such as recidivism amongst ex-offenders. For instance, CEO posits that if a person with a conviction can find employment after they are first released or after conviction, then "they will be less likely to become reincarcerated and more likely to build a foundation for a stable, productive life for themselves and their families."[14] The appropriate intervention is therefore assistance in finding a job, which could include life skills training and work experience, and the desired impact is both to place as many individuals as possible and to encourage those in work to stay there. For instance, CEO has placed nearly 25,000 ex-offenders in almost a decade.[15]

Founded in 1981, the DC organization is part of a network of social projects established and run largely by members of a local church. The founder of the organization has remained as director. At the time of the research in the late nineties, there were twelve paid staff, including a number of former service users. Founded in 2011, the Manchester initiative has only two staff members and has worked with a much smaller service user population, about 420 in all, with about half placed in jobs. Housed in the city's cathedral, the project's existence symbolizes the engagement of the Church of England in championing the rights of low-income families and individuals during an era of austerity and its more specific encouragement of grassroots social action and local innovation.

The services of the DC organization consist of a counseling service to prepare for and find a job, and for those in jobs for four months or longer, guidance on how to improve life opportunities, whether through education, vocational training, or other changes, such as new housing. With both organizations, as well as others like Goodwill and Pecan, service users may not have the skills to qualify for white-collar, clerical jobs or access work in trades like plumbing or carpentry. They also may have just left prison or ceased to receive welfare benefits and are thus negotiating the psychological consequences of 'de-institutionalization' or (re-)learning to work, as well as childcare responsibilities and most importantly, the multiple challenges of poverty. Some are also facing problems of addiction and domestic violence, as well as mental illness.

The research on the two projects, despite their different locations and time periods, took place during periods of profound transformation in welfare policy, or the late nineties in the United States and since 2010 in the United Kingdom. Despite facing similar cuts to benefits, as well as political stigmatization of welfare recipients (associated with TANF), the organization in DC had trouble placing clients in jobs that offered significant opportunities for social mobility and greater income, or simply non-exploitative conditions, whereas the project in Manchester succeeded in placing perhaps even more vulnerable service users in stable posts. Inverting the conclusions of Ramanath's path-dependency analysis—or the effects of organizational characteristics on responses to external pressures, I will suggest that the difference in the conception of the problem, service, and impact reflects external constraints. These include the DC organization's membership within a church-based network of social projects, with accompanying performance expectations and politics; the reputation of the organization for delivering a 'placement' service; and the lack of local employers willing to hire the clients of the DC organization, who are often ex-offenders or former welfare recipients. Furthermore, as with CEO, Pecan, and other organizations, the placement service complements political rhetoric and policy stressing the need for welfare recipients to find work. At the same time, the Manchester project benefits from unique assets such as the Church of England's critique of austerity and access to the contacts of the cathedral.

In addressing employability, the Manchester initiative has striven to offer an explicitly distinctive approach, or one based on relationship building rather than personal transformation as a cause and effect of finding a job. For instance, the DC organization states that productivity of a job breaks the isolation of unemployment. The Manchester project instead concentrates on expressing respect for the individual and developing a network of support, including with local employers, particularly at an executive level. Job placement targets, whether in charities or government agencies like Job Centres in the United Kingdom, and the impersonal nature of government social services are regarded as part of the problem, because they undermine the social relations, or trust, and recognition of individual dignity necessary to make changes in complicated lives. For the organization, "quality relationships, not ticks in boxes make the difference," "people helping people" is effective, and "choice and free will achieves outcomes."[16] The organization's staff will always be available to help, or provide a reliable, trustworthy source of support. The organization advertises its service as having "no goodbyes, we have time for you no matter what." As with Goodwill and CEO, though not with the DC organization, the program provides volunteering experience at the cathedral to increase skills and self-confidence. To promote the sense of individual agency and self-respect, men and women using the job placement service are called 'volunteers' and not 'clients' or 'customers.' The intention of the service is for it to be "their own decision to choose and commit to being a volunteer."[17]

In the research, the difference in approaches to employment had implications for how service users and staff interacted, and arguably for capacity to intervene or support individuals either unhappy in their current jobs or searching for a better position, or both. The majority of jobs available to clients at the time of research in DC were minimum wage, without benefits (for the first three months), and far from where the clients lived (see Newman 2008; Ehrenreich 2001; Wilson 1996; Smith et al. 2014). These jobs were often at fast food restaurants, grocery stores, and retail shops. Clients worked as busboys, cleaners, servers, and checkers. Occasionally, clients would secure jobs at call centers, nursing homes, or apartment complexes, where they would perform odd maintenance jobs.

Despite a push at the time from the director to promote 'move-up' jobs for clients who had stayed in a position for longer than six months, counselors doubted they could find better positions for the majority of clients because of their low skill levels. They also felt reluctant to offer false promises of finding higher paying work for men and women holding on to mediocre jobs. Clients did not remain in jobs for a variety of reasons:

poor employment conditions, family constraints, difficulties adjusting to a work schedule, or conflicts with supervisors. Tensions with supervisors figured prominently into reasons for dismissal or leaving a job, and likewise reflected the structural constraint on job mobility among clients. From the perspective of clients, supervisors abused the workplace hierarchy and overreacted to mistakes. New hires were easy scapegoats if something at work had gone wrong. For instance, one supervisor blamed a crisis on a client of mine, complaining that she "had an attitude. These people have street attitudes."[18] Even the most motivated clients felt they were subject to discrimination because of their backgrounds, namely lack of skills and sometimes, criminal record. An older client told me,

> I have to stay in my job because I am the head of the household. If I don't pay my rent, no one is going to pay it. A lot of people I talk to live with someone who pays the rent. They don't have the responsibility to pay for food and eating. I have to stay in my job because if I don't, I won't have a roof.[19]

In an initial conversation, she commented that she accepted the workplace hierarchy:

> The experience you have, you have to take it and do it the way they want it done. A co-worker with more restaurant experience than I have . . . felt she was too qualified, but you still have to prove yourself. Not everybody is cut out to be a manager, but that does not mean you can't earn more money.

She also had the patience to accommodate customers and the experience of how to please supervisors:

> You have to forget the word 'No.' You never tell a customer 'No.' And you have to be busy all the time. Managers don't like to walk past and see that you are just standing there. They do not like to you to stand there. I picked that up at Fresh Fields. You have to find something to do.

Yet, in a second interview, months later, she talked to me about quitting her job. "They treat you like a dog," she said angrily.

> If I didn't have this apartment to pay for, I would have told him what I think. I would have walked out if the rent was not $450/month. But I have

done all I could do with this one. I have never missed a day and never been late. He [the supervisor] treats me like a dog.

Talking to me about the job placement organization, she remarked sharply, "You send people on jobs but you don't realize what they do."

The challenge for counselors, however, was not just in convincing clients to remain in a difficult, occasionally abusive position until they could find another post but also in persuading supervisors to moderate their behavior and possess more patience, namely to restrain from dismissing employees the organization had sent them. Unfortunately for the most part, supervisors were as outspoken in their criticism of clients' behavior as clients were of the disrespect they felt supervisors showed them. A manager at a business that frequently hired clients told me she wanted applicants prepared to conform and express motivation. She then cited an employee from the organization who had moved up into a better job but was also at risk of losing it. "She needs an attitude class," the manager remarked. "She is very negative, very vocal about what she likes and does not like. She needs to understand what appropriate behaviour is. It is ok to ask questions but in a certain way."[20] Another manager at an apartment complex was even more severe of her assessment of several of the clients. One, she complained, "did not look you directly in the eye." "It could be a cultural thing," she added. She concluded our conversation with a comment about two employees that she had fired: "I wouldn't recommend these people to anyone."[21]

Supervisors were quick to distinguish between promising and unacceptable job applicants, categorizing them according to self-motivation and compliance. The supervisor of an assistant manager who had come from the organization complimented his work ethic and performance. The supervisor described the assistant manager as "hungry" and remarked that he attained his position because he "stepped up to the plate when we wanted him to." On the other hand, they were both disparaging about the overwhelming majority of applicants that came from the organization.[22] "They don't know how to fill out an application. They leave no references or job contacts," the assistant manager lamented. "They don't seem interested in finding a job. They don't seem enthusiastic. 'Whatever' is their attitude," he said. He told me that they could not explain their last job or tell him what they wanted to do in the future. "They say they are just looking for a job instead of giving me a five-year plan."

When I asked why employees from the organization did not last long, he responded, "because of their work ethic, they steal, there are integrity issues." The difference between him and these applicants, he commented, "Is that I am a go-getter. I know this is a stepping-stone." At the time I interviewed him, in 1999, the assistant manager had interviewed about fifty applicants sent by the organization over three years. He had hired about ten, or a fifth. On average, they had stayed about a year, though he stated as well that he had let go about eight out of ten because "they took food, juice. . . . If you see there is nothing you can do, then you have to let them go. The organization's applicants are no different from the others."

The common lore among counselors was that clients who had found stable jobs did so only at other charitable, typically faith-based, organizations sympathetic to their pasts and their efforts to overcome them (see Perlmutter et al. 2005). The 'star' client for the organization was the manager at a rehabilitation center that belonged to the same church as the job placement organization. Indeed, when I interviewed staff at local nonprofit organizations, such as labor unions or foundations, I generally encountered reluctance or resistance to become engaged with clients, with the exception of one labor union possessing a majority African American membership. A representative of another labor union desperate for younger members informed me that she was afraid of potential drug use, and that she had heard that Ethiopians were reliable and honest (compared to African Americans). A staff member of a think tank known for its work on poverty commented, "We need to put our money where our mouth is. We talk about poverty a lot but we have not directly done something within our own organization."[23] However, she thought our clients would require too much time and training to acquire the necessary clerical skills to work in an office environment. "If [the organization] has an exceptionally educated client, we would think about it," she told me. A staff member of another organization in DC bluntly summed up the structural difficulties clients faced and the lack of support they had to overcome these difficulties. She told me,

> The government just wants them to get a job. They can pretty it up but they just want them to get a job. A woman who has five kids who works at McDonald's can't pay for day care, housing. I think it stinks. I think it is set up so that there will always be an underclass, there will always be people who eat bad food, who take the jobs nobody wants.

Like the DC organization, the Manchester project has placed some of its volunteers in 'easy' positions, such as the cathedral's café. At the same time, the director, who also works in the development office of the cathedral, has found local employers willing to hire project participants in jobs with potential. He explained that personal contact, or building relations with local employers, helped. "Nobody thinks about it when trying to find jobs. They don't think about talking to a real person. I just picked up the phone and called the executive." Subsequently, the organization has succeeded in placing participants in jobs that have led to promotion, for instance, to a café manager. Continued contact with staff and other volunteers has meant that individuals can rely upon support while in a job or return to volunteering, keeping their involvement in the workplace, if the job does not work out.

In conclusion, the effectiveness of the Manchester project in both job placement and retention can be attributed to a combination of the attention to trust and relationships rather than outputs (number of job placements); the director's motivation and position of authority within the cathedral and the city; the profile, mission, and resources of the cathedral itself; and employer interest in being involved. At the same time, the DC organization has survived for more than thirty-five years, in part by offering the same kind of recognizable and easily understood service, particularly by donors, with quantifiable impact. The DC organization's approach predominates because on one level, it complements policy objectives and employer incentive to maintain a flexible, low-wage workforce and, on another, produces an easily replicated service that makes the individual–rather than a collective body, which is harder to maintain–responsible for both personal and broader social change.

Correspondence and Discrepancies Between Organizations and the State

Analyzing differences and commonalities in how policymakers and public institutions on the one hand, and charities on the other, understand need can expose the challenges of effective intervention and demonstrate how conflict and cooperation with institutions and/or other external actors influence the constitution and reproduction of the field (Young

2000). The conception of the social problem binding a field across organizations and individuals can affect the characteristics of organizations cited previously, such as sustainability, public profile, and social networks. This effect is noticeable when outliers, like the Manchester Cathedral project, offer alternative conceptions and are not easily replicated. Differences between organizations and external actors like public institutions in defining the problem can, on the other hand, affect the dynamism and evolution of the field, as it may remain fixed on an oppositional stance to policy and institutional behavior. Services essentially become political advocacy, with subsequent consequences for internal issues like resource management and staff motivation and self-identity and external relations, as policymakers and institutions may demonstrate little interest in helping the field to survive (unlike job placement services, for instance).

Denis Young (2000) uses a comparison between nonprofit organizations in the United States, United Kingdom, Japan, and Israel to outline three types of relationships with public sector agencies: supplementary, complementary, and adversarial (151). In other words, they can offer services conventionally provided by the public sector, they can enhance public services by providing needed and missing interventions, and they can act—particularly as advocates for vulnerable groups—to correct or reform public services. For example, similar to Appropriate Adults, the field of educational advocacy for children with special needs is derived from legislation. Like AA, the service protects and implements legal rights. The desired impact for organizations, however, is not just to provide representation—which in the case of Appropriate Adults, everyone agrees upon—but also improved school support. In fact, advocates identify the 'problem' addressed by their services as differing interpretations of legally required school support. The Washington, DC organization Advocates for Justice and Education, Inc. describes its founding purpose as confronting "the grave injustices and denial of basic special education services, and to educate parents, and those working with parents about the laws that govern special education and related services."[24] The organization also strives to raise public awareness of the "judicial consequences that results from educational institutions' negligence and inappropriate classification of students with special needs," namely, the (costly) legal challenges that arise because of school actions.[25]

The disagreement between advocates and the school system is based on language in national legislation, which cite school responsibility to ensure 'adequate education,' and thus do not technically mandate 'maximization' of a child's potential learning ability. For instance, in detailing the regulatory requirements for identifying children with disabilities, the Individuals with Disabilities Improved Education Act (IDEA) states that one consideration is that "The child does not achieve adequately for the child's age or to meet State-approved grade-level standards" and another is that "The child does not make sufficient progress to meet age or State-approved grade-level standards"[26] (IDEA 2004). Therefore, if the school system wants to resist paying for specialized services for disabled students, then they can use the language of 'adequate' and 'sufficient' to deny entitlement. If a child is passing from one grade to another or is performing at an average level, then the school system may claim it has no mandate to help the child progress further. Or the school can provide a service but then not extend it after a period of time based on 'adequate' academic performance.

During a short research trip to Washington, DC in 2009, I interviewed a number of advocates and educational lawyers working for low-income parents of children with special needs who attended local public schools. They told me that they spent much of their time negotiating with public school staff members over entitlement to supplementary educational services or threatening legal action. The lawyers consistently saw themselves as lone champions fighting the state. One longtime education lawyer summarized her reputation: "I am not seen as a friend [within the DC School District]. I am seen as a pain in the butt."[27] Like other advocates, she thought that the laws themselves were sufficient. For her, acts like No Child Left Behind (2002), The Individuals with Disabilities Education Act (1997), The Individuals with Disabilities Improved Education Act (2004), and the recent Every Student Succeeds Act (2016) have established or clarified the rights of disabled children to the same education as non-disabled children. The difficulty, the lawyer explained, was that she "had to hold people's hands to the fire" in the DC school system. "While people respect what I do in the system, they don't like it because it costs them money. I ask them to provide the service kids are entitled to or I ask them to pay for it privately."

The education lawyer's view, cynical and blunt, was that "School Districts have made the decision to fight like tigers to intimidate parents rather than to admit that they have to provide a service." She added that "Some School Districts go to great expense to prevent children from getting services parents want them to get." She explained that parents with resources will seek evaluations outside the school system which state, "your son or daughter need x, y, and z. Parents then take the report to the school system, which says we don't have to provide that." She provided one example of a double amputee not receiving special education services because his academic performance remained 'average' and his disability did not fit into any of the categories. Another example was of a blind student taught in Braille who possessed a cognitive impairment, hindering her in turn from understanding Braille. Yet, the district saw her as 'blind' and therefore in need of Braille.

Her legal strategy was to see if the school district made procedural violations that she could bring up in negotiations or during a hearing. For instance, in the case of twins with Down's syndrome, the district should have drafted a plan to facilitate the transition between preschool and elementary school. However, the school had failed to do so, and faced with the lapse, the parents put the twins in private nursery. They then asked the lawyer to pursue reimbursement based on the district's error. A similar case involved a child with autism. The district offered the parents a place in a preschool class where the teacher came from Teach for America, a program for college graduates to teach in schools in low-income areas for two years. Inexperienced in general, the teacher was not qualified to work with autistic kids. The parents, like the ones in the previous example, refused to put their child in the class and thus paid for a private nursery. Like the other parents as well, they asked the lawyer to pursue reimbursement from the district for offering inadequate education.

Echoing the anger and dismay of the lawyer, a senior case worker at an educational charity spoke of her frustration in that "nothing had changed in twenty years." She lamented that "I am not any happier than when I started.[28] What I see the system doing is cutting costs." For her, cutting costs "has been the effort and the commitment [from schools]." Schools followed the logic that, "If we can insist that the kid does a, b, and c rather than x, y, and z, then we will cut costs." Her conclusion, however, was that the strategy was counterproductive: "I think they [DC school district personnel] create problems for themselves. It costs them more. We have to go through the legal process and they have to provide for private school."

Despite a history of making expensive procedural errors, the power of the school district as the service provider easily eclipsed the meager resources and social marginality that characterized most low-income families seeking services. Some parents possess low levels of education and little knowledge of English. They may also face other crises, such as termination of benefits or health problems without insurance, and personal problems, namely domestic violence and drug use. In fact, the education lawyer criticized schools for taking advantage of families unaware of legislation and their rights. She accused the school system of "milking the jargon to the nth degree" because they knew that "parents are too embarrassed to admit they don't know the jargon that employees use." She said, "I have parents come in all of the time who come with a school report that they don't understand."[29]

In addition to individual school resistance, advocates and parents have faced national policy and the DC (and other) school system restrictions on reimbursement for legal fees, in effect dissuading parents and law firms from pursuing legal challenges. IDEA (2004) forbids awarding attorneys' fees "for services performed subsequent to a written offer of settlement, under specified conditions" and allows for "a reduction of award of attorneys' fees under certain circumstances, including where the parent or parent's attorney unreasonably protracted the final resolution of the controversy" (Vacca 2007: 2). The capacity to shift the cost of fees to the family or reduce attorney in DC may be difficult in court[30] but the DC school district (DCPS) has pursued the legal cap of $90 an hour for representing special needs cases. At the time I conducted research in 2009, DCPS, supported by congressional legislation (2003), had set a $4,000 limit on fee claims,[31] though the cap was later lifted by 2009 legislation.[32] Regardless, lawyers representing families must weigh the cost of the case against other work. A lawsuit between a firm representing a number of cases and DCPS, which arrived at $1.8 million settlement, displayed the persistent tensions between firms, and families, and the school district. A legal blog for the capital recounts how, "The Brown firm . . . laid off 21 of its 32 attorneys and support staff, blaming the city's failure to pay fees."[33] For the field, the more pernicious implication is its volatility and unsustainability, or that future involvement of legal services will be limited if the problem remains rooted in the absence of cooperation and agreement.

That said, in the research, not all interactions between advocates and schools were confrontational. If representation of pupils with special needs seems increasingly too expensive for law firms, nonprofit engagement at a school level could be effective. One advocate, not a lawyer, who worked for a local nonprofit organization, estimated that about half of her relationships with school staff were 'collaborative.' The other half she described as 'oppositional.' She claimed, "I generally have positive relationships unless the person is trying to get away with something." She said that some school staff would call her surreptitiously to encourage her to advocate. "They can't do it because their job is on the line. Their superior will be upset."[34] Indeed, the education lawyer complained that staff showing up at hearings would be 'forgetful' because of pressure from their supervisors and fear about their jobs.

A former advocate at an organization assisting kindergarten through high school students to access educational support told me her first task at each school was to find the person responsible for special education because the post seemed to have a different title wherever she went.[35] She explained that, "A huge part of what I did was building relationships because at the beginning generally I was met with a negative response. Most of the time, I would go in and it would be 'who is the white gal?'" She added, "This was not just about color, but because they [the teachers] would want to make sure that I wasn't going to make their lives more difficult." Their antagonism was also due to their desire to avoid talking through an intermediary to the 'Mom.' She would try quickly to negate their fears. "I would say, 'I am here to make your life easier. If we arrange an appointment, I will pick up Mom from work instead of her having to take a couple of busses to make it here.'" The retreat of firms like the one mentioned above and the positive effect of relationship building may mean that the 'problem' remains the same but the methods of intervention become focused on supporting parents to become more assertive in their children's current schools. For instance, Advocates for Justice and Education works to 'empower' families through training and support groups, as well as legal representation. The case worker quoted above also felt that the legal resolution of children leaving the mainstream school system for private or charter schools may be impractical and potentially destructive. For her, the better charter schools were not in low-income areas and likewise, the private schools were 'far away.' Children with special needs would thus have to travel to get to school. For a field rooted in the 'adversarial' relationship of Young (2000), the future may be working within the system.

What Happens When Organizations Change Their Mind About Their Services?

The third question interrogates the rationale for altering conceptions of a social problem and subsequently the services, and examines the consequences of these decisions to the organization. Both the change in conception and the effect on the organization reveal the specific obstacles and the more profound complexity in transforming a field. Another organization in Washington, DC involved in education, in this case mentoring high school students, offers an example of the trials and risk of failure that defining the social problem differently presents. I conducted research with this organization in 2003–2004.

The organization belonged to the same network of church-based initiatives as the job placement organization mentioned previously. To mentor effectively students in a relatively low-income area, the organizations had to negotiate local politics of school management, an overburdened DC school system unable to coordinate with tutoring programs about the needs of specific students, intense competition for relatively small amounts of private funding,[36] and the minimal political, social, and material resources available to teenage children of low-income, minority, often immigrant families. One aim of the organization was to transfer comparatively high-performing students and students facing problems, and sometimes violence, at their own school to charter schools. Staff members therefore were also working to find places, even at charter schools that were far away (in some cases where the problems were related to gang violence, this was the intention).

The organization's services when the director arrived resembled those of larger mentoring organizations in the United States and elsewhere. When he had first arrived in the late nineties, the organization offered a drop-in center for teenagers desiring help at school. The service was run by two adult tutors helping approximately forty teenagers. Responding to what he saw as superficial or insignificant results, he altered the service to demand more commitment from teenagers over a year-long period. At the same time, he hired more staff as team leaders for three groups of about eight teenagers each. He also wanted the organization to function as a mediator between two of the most important institutions in the area, families and the school system, where little to no relationship existed. To do this, he set as goals transferring schools if they could not address student needs and parental concerns and more abstractly, the teenage mentees developing through discipline and adult guidance optimism about life opportunities.

The intensiveness of the new service and its direct engagement with school administrations, often *in locum parentis*, differed from other mentoring services. For instance, the national organization Big Brothers, Big Sisters (BBBS) in the United States, which works in about 330 communities around the country, matches adults with children and teenagers who "need us most, including those living in single parent homes, growing up in poverty and coping with parental incarceration."[37] Volunteer mentors should expect to spend several hours a month with their mentees participating in activities ranging from going to a museum to sports. Mentors can also meet in the mentees' schools for shared activities. The aims of a program like that of BBBS also include improved academic performance and more generally, better life choices, such as resisting drug use and violence. At least one evaluation (Tierney et al. 2000) has demonstrated that the program has had a positive impact on academic performance and behavior in and out of school.

For the director, however, this kind of service was insufficient in addressing the problems teenagers confronted at home and in school. The service he subsequently designed also consisted of finding mentors for teenagers, but mentees had to commit to after-school tutoring classes at the organization, introducing in effect a selection process, and to allowing project staff to represent them at their schools. In exchange, mentors and project staff would provide adult support and help the teenager shift to another school.

The intensity of the program also entailed hiring more staff, who could provide additional support to mentees when needed. In an interview, he laughed as he recounted his tenure at the organization, "The joke around here is that since I showed up, we have doubled our staff and halved our numbers."[38] For him, no single adult in the mentees' lives could adequately provide the support teenagers in vulnerable circumstances needed to improve school performance and make decisions to widen life opportunities. The staff created circles of adults composed of the mentor, the organization staff, the parents, and the school counselor. The circle would maintain a flow of information about the teenager, decide on a plan for their immediate and longer-term future, and intervene when necessary. He told me,

> It is really hard for our kids to have the kind of structure and have the degree of follow-through [to pursue a better education]. If you choose to pursue a better school, suddenly you have a lot of work to do. And the families are not going to be around to help. You have to fill in that form, do that question, and that is where the staff come in.

Though respectful of parents, the director clearly thought the teenagers at his center required additional adult supervision:

> Parents are not free enough to be supportive enough. Sometimes it is work. They are gone all the time when kids are at home. Sometimes, it is education. They never learned to read beyond fifth-grade level or dropped out. Maybe they are from El Salvador and never went beyond a certain level. And their kids are growing up here so they can't understand. So there is only so much they can do to help with education. And poverty is exhausting. Their personal resources are not there to help a kid, to hold him accountable when he is resisting. It takes a tremendous amount of energy.

He added,

> Whatever the particular constellation in a specific instance, poverty, the parent is struggling with their own issues, we want to a) free parents up; and b) support them from wherever they are at. If they are a junkie, they are not really there for their kids, but wherever they are, we will form a group of support and accountability for the teenager.

As a consequence, the project required parents of the teenagers to sign an information release in order to give the organization access to student records and to become involved with the schools. The degree of intervention depended of course on the teenager's performance in school as well as the interest of the mentor.

To achieve the impact he wanted, or creating better life opportunities, the director instated rules for participation. He wanted only the teenagers already demonstrating ambition and commitment to remain as mentees:

> [Before] We were mostly running around putting out fires.... [W]e still get about forty kids floating around that we are involved with in some way or another, but of them, only about thirty get registered, and of them, only about twenty-four, twenty-five will stick it out for the year.... We said, "choose what you are going to choose and let's not play games now. You can't have one foot in and one foot out. Choose. If you can't be in here, be out there. We are always here for you to come back to. Whenever you are ready."

As the manager had predicted and wanted, the teenagers possessing the will to persist stayed while the others left. He recalled that the transformation of the service helped some while dissuading others:

> [The change] enabled some to really step forward, start making some strides and growing. It also meant that a lot of kids didn't feel like dealing with it.... We had a girl who didn't want to do reading after school but she was a few years behind. We told her there is no reading teacher in the school, in any DC high school, so you are going to have to do it here. You say you want to go to college, right? But she got angry and stormed out and traipsed around a little bit and told the kids, "while you are inside doing your reading and writing, I am going to be outside playing tag." And there you have it. That is pretty much everyone's choice right now.

By setting examples of resistant participants, the director in effect set boundaries, excluding those whom he felt would not change their behavior.

In contrast to his sensitivity toward parents and optimism about remaining participants, the director was cynical, even disparaging of the interest of schools in the welfare of their students.[39] He commented that he had seen students come to the center to cut and paste from the internet in writing an assignment. Shocked when student would return with Bs or Cs for obviously plagiarized homework, he sighed,

> What a teacher sees from a student who has cut and pasted a paper, this is someone who has bothered to go to the internet so that becomes the curve.

> So I don't think they are supported. Teachers aren't judged by how much contact they have with their students or understand their circumstances. They just have to get through their day.

When he elaborated upon his relationship with the school system, he grew more emotional:

> Basically, schools don't know their kids. It is amazing how disconnected adults are from their kids' lives. Teachers are disconnected and parents are disconnected from the teachers. What kids need is to be inspired, to be known for who they are, the good and bad, to be cared about and loved, to fail at things, to screw up, and to be held accountable for it but not loved any less, to be reminded to make a choice, 'you screwed up, you go off track, welcome to the human race.' The question is do you want to keep going down that path, do you want to continue to fuck up, do you want to be a fuck-up? It means loving them enough to say that.

He cited school disinterest and parent distance from schools as justification for changing the service, despite its cost and reduction in numbers,

> We need a web of adults communicating about a kid. . . . What kids need is someone to fill in the gaps like a parent does. That does not happen. Everyone is doing well-intentioned, good, useful things, but it is in isolation. Meantime, the kids keep slipping through everyone's cracks and people wonder why.

When the service succeeded, it provided entirely new options. The director claimed,

> For the vast majority of kids stuck in the public school system, there is no possibility of getting them out. But for each kid who gets out [to attend a private or charter school], they suddenly have a new lease on life.

However, the organization had trouble finding mentors who could provide the kind of personal connection they were seeking between an adult mentor and the teenager. The director also could not depend upon the parent church for more funding and human resources because church-based organizations already offered two other mentoring services for different age groups. In 2007, the church hired an accountant to shut down the organization, as it was deemed financially unsustainable.

In terms of analyzing the field of mentoring, the organization's ambitions and subsequent demise could reflect poor strategic planning but they could also indicate lack of available funding and political and institutional interest, in this case on the part of school administrations, in change. The factors cited previously, such as expectations of service from particular organizations, organizational relations with policymakers and funding bodies, and internal management characteristics (the founder still in place as executive director), help maintain types of services with particular aims. At the same time, the intensive dimension of the organization's services require a financial commitment and a disregard for numerical outputs, and thus ultimately, a different understanding of what a charity in the field should achieve. The prominent thinker on evaluation, Michael Scriven (2016), describes how fixation on what charities in a field should accomplish can occlude what charities need to accomplish, in this case facilitate creating new life opportunities for disadvantaged youth. He writes about how, "if program theory only means the theory the program people believe is operative, it's sometimes not so hard to produce it, though not trivial since the designers' program theory may no longer be the one the managers believe in, let alone the field workers" (42). Worse still, he argues, is if "it's only the believed theory, then of course, it will be of little help for you, or the client, in pointing the way toward problem spots or side-effects." Scriven (2016) The side effects for the director were motivated and disciplined teenagers not receiving enough support or explicit intervention in schools from a conventional mentoring program. The failure to find an alternative reveals the stability and simultaneously, the limitations of the field.

Altering Fields

Scriven's intention is to raise recognition for evaluation as a discipline, rather than a practical add-on or a source of anxiety for scholars distrusting assessment measures. He notes that evaluators may not and do not necessarily need to understand how a service produces impact. However, if organizations want the right program theory, "that is, one that explains what actually has happened," Scriven notes, "then you need to find out what that is—including all the good and bad results—before you can determine what caused the outcomes, that is, the program theory. That means you have to do the evaluation first, not after you cook up the theory" (2016: 37). Assessing and transforming an area of work, or a field of social action, also entails understanding the consequences of delivering services, but this assessment includes analyzing the effects of conceptualizing the social problem itself in a particular way. What information has been left out in identifying a problem? For instance, can the problem be described as insufficiently supportive, personal interaction between teenagers and responsible adults? Or should the problem be considered as more complex, including inadequate representation within the institutions, like schools, associated with teenagers from a disadvantaged background, and lack of necessary intervention to create better life choices?

Transitional housing projects offer an example of how to analyze and transform a field in a specific context. While working in DC in 2000–2004 at George Washington University in their Human Services program (in the Department of Sociology), I conducted research with several transitional housing projects. I have also conducted more recent research (2014–2015) in London with night shelters, though of course, they only provide emergency housing. Both types of programs rely on legal definitions of homelessness in accepting service users. For instance, the American HEARTH Act (2009) replicates and expands upon four categories of homelessness established in the earlier McKinney-Vento Homeless Assistance Act (1987):

> (1) Individuals and families who lack a fixed, regular, and adequate nighttime residence and includes a subset for an individual who resided in an emergency shelter or a place not meant for human habitation and who is exiting an institution where he or she temporarily resided; (2) individuals and families who will imminently lose their primary nighttime residence; (3) unaccompanied youth and families with children and youth who are defined as homeless under other federal statutes who do not otherwise qualify as homeless under this definition; and (4) individuals and families who are fleeing, or are attempting to flee, domestic violence, dating violence, sexual assault, stalking, or other dangerous or life-threatening conditions that relate to violence against the individual or a family member.[40]

One of the causes of homelessness established by Congress in the Hearth Act is "a lack of affordable housing and limited scale of housing assistance programs."[41] Indeed, when I interviewed the director of a transitional housing program in DC, before the Hearth Act, he said, "My plan for addressing the homeless problem would be one, invest a lot of money to prevent people from getting into the system in the first place." He added, "The shelter system is very expensive. There are a lot of people here who don't need the support of the system. They are pretty high functioning people. You could just subsidize their rent."[42]

However, organizations helping the homeless focus primarily on the return to housing, and not prevention. As Home Aid America notes in its description of the 10 causes of homelessness, these organizations coordinate with other service providers to "provide the services, such as job training, social skills training, and financial training, that enable these people to regain employment and return to mainstream lives."[43] The objective of the director's transitional housing project was to move families into permanent housing.

At the time, the program possessed twenty units. The director discussed with me how he would negotiate with the representative from the Community Partnership, a nonprofit organization that coordinates services for the city concerning homelessness, over moving families out of transitional housing. The representative would encourage shelters to enforce the six-month time limit on sheltered housing. The director told me that officially, "Our objective is that 60% of our families will move into stable housing. We well superseded that the year before last [2001] by having 86% of our families move into stable housing." Yet, reaching this objective depended, logically, on availability, especially for larger families (a parent with four or more children). For most families in sheltered housing, stable housing meant accessing Housing Choice Vouchers, which provide a rent subsidy paid directly to landlords of housing the families find on their own.[44]

The director explained to me that

> By law, this is a six-month maximum program. There is another law that says they don't move until there is a place for them to go. That is the provision that keeps people here for a long time. The major factor is family size. Big families stay. The second factor is substance abuse. There are a few Section 8 Vouchers [Housing Choice Vouchers] trickling out, but nowhere near the demand.

He then discussed the implications of the contradiction in policy:

> The problem is what the Community Partnership would like us to do, which I refuse to do, is to say how many people will that be [moving out], how many families will that be. I will not assume the responsibility moving a certain amount of families out when there is no place for them to go. And our numbers decreased dramatically last year. The year before we moved out 24 families. Last year we moved out 14. . . . In terms of what I am promising I will do for them, I am not going to promise I will move out a certain number of families because there is nowhere to go. I am not going to put myself on the line like that. They do [put pressure on me]. I try to ignore it. I think about our guy at Partnership, we go to meetings and it is "You got to move families out, y'all not moving families out." [And I say] "Where are they going to go?" It is ridiculous. Sometimes they will say, "We know how hard it is, we know there is no place for them to go" and so on.

The difficulty of moving families out of homelessness has continued to the extent that the number of families in emergency shelter and transitional housing is now greater than the number of individuals. Among the 6,259 persons staying in emergency shelters that were counted in the Point In Time (PIT) annual survey of homelessness in DC, 2,594 were alone and 3,665 were part of 1,136 families. In the count of persons in transitional housing, 771 were unaccompanied and 1,002 were part of 355 families.[45] At the time of the 2016 survey, the overall number of homeless persons had increased 14.4% from 2015, though the number of unaccompanied individuals had decreased by 3.8%. The number of families had driven the rise, increasing by 31.8%. The trend is not a one-off, as other analyses, such as that by the DC homeless support service organization So Others May Eat (SOME), have shown dramatic increases in the number of homeless families, including a 38.1% rise between 2009 and 2013.[46]

In considering homeless services as a field, I suggest that rather than focusing primarily on responses like the availability of social or low-cost housing,[47] it may be more beneficial to reconceptualize the social problem itself. The emphasis on defining homelessness and identifying and consolidating services available to this population, as detailed in policy like the HEARTH Act, means that efforts are directed at and assessed, as suggested in the director's previous comments, by moving people back into permanent housing as quickly as possible (the HEARTH Act has a thirty-days target). Yet, is the problem homelessness or precarity, uncertainty in which inadequate public services, work opportunities, and income support, as well as access to affordable housing, combine to push people into losing their homes? Should services cover a much wider population and combination of needs, with the aim of overcoming precarity? As precarity is generated by personal problems and external pressures, such as rising rent or temporary contracts, should activities aim to foster communication between different actors, such as landlords, tenants, counselors, and employers, and different social groups, namely those in various states of precarity? The SOME analysis discussed earlier cites statistics in the 2013 DC PIT, where lack of income is identified as one of the most significant causes of homelessness. In the PIT, "[Forty-five percent] of unaccompanied adults and 18% of adults in families reported that they had no income of any kind." Moreover, among adults in families, only 25% were in employment (Chapman et al. 2013: 43).

The intent of translating precarity into social action differs from a theory of political mobilization (Standing 2014, 2011) or a call for political resistance. Guy Standing, in a considerable body of work, discussed how the precariat is a class in formation, based on flexible, exploitative working conditions and decreasing relative pay to hours of labor. He writes that, "the precariat must perform a growing and high ratio of work-for-labour to labour itself. It is exploited as much off the workplace and outside remunerated hours of labour as in it" (2014: 3). In other words, people, particularly those without advanced skills and high levels of education, must look hard for work, regardless of pay and conditions. This competition exacerbates their insecurity. States, for Standing, show little interest in protecting this population, instead gradually stripping their rights and denying what have been the attributes of citizenship, at least post-War in Western countries. Standing states, "This is the first time in history when the state is systematically taking away rights from its own citizens. . . . They are increasingly denied what Hannah Arendt called 'the right to have rights,' the essence of proper citizenship" (2014: 4).

Indeed, the SOME analysis argues that "the first thing" homeless people need in DC "is to be treated with respect and dignity. Homeless persons are individuals with life stories to tell" (2013). The appropriate policy response and likewise, the development of social interventions effective at instigating life changes should reflect this attitude. Housing programs like mixed-income developments, where housing is made available to residents of different income and social backgrounds, seemingly adopt this principle. The theory is that combining provision of stable housing with exposure to 'middle class' families and individuals will generate personal transformation, as the wealthier residents offer social networks and examples of values and success and increase demand for proper property and management and availability of high quality goods and services (Joseph 2006; Joseph et al. 2015). However, setting up a structure to support interaction does not necessarily address the complexity of needs among low-income residents, who have faced the stress and pressures of poverty and instability, or mean more generally that residents of different backgrounds will form relationships.

In his review of the assumptions and impact of mixed-income developments in the United States, Joseph (2006) argues that these developments alone cannot produce change, but rather have to be linked with greater investment in social services, education, job placement, transportation, and skill development (223). As importantly, residents need to feel they are part of a community, where they can trust others. Joseph et al. (2015) note in a later analysis of mixed-income developments in San Francisco that "experience has shown that community building needs to be integrated into service connection, because community building supports trusting relationships with service connectors—and without trust, on-site staff cannot work effectively with families." Returning to precarity, an obstacle to increasing trust is the unstable working conditions of service workers themselves (Baines et al. 2014; Light 2003). Examining conditions in Canada for nonprofit staff, Baines et al. point to how this instability, caused by contracting and funding cuts, especially in the public sector, undermines service continuity. They write, "Cut to the bone, nonprofits find it increasingly challenging to maintain, let alone to strengthen, community connections" (2014: 78). The personal effect is that social service workers often share with service users the same sense of precariousness (84), perhaps especially if they have come from a similar background.

Re-conceptualizing the social problem as precarity, or insecurity, within a field of social action can address the challenges facing both staff and service users in a continuum of service provision and participation and link a collective identity or category of shared experience with practical intervention. Rethinking the social problem should also affect the reflexive position of organizations, whereby, as Emirbayer and Williams (2005) note, social service workers comprehend better

> the external forces assigning, as it were, to their particular case some of its pertinent properties. It can also give them comparative purchase on the sometimes bewildering complexities, challenges, and difficulties, seemingly so very idiosyncratic, of the cases that they seek to tackle.
>
> (2005: 718)

Moreover, this comprehension allows for organizational leaders and staff to relate their own power and resources within a field to 'external forces' and likewise, how reassessing the 'problem' can counter these forces and alter their own position.

On a more practical level, identifying precarity as a social problem to address through social services means tying together services typically linked to vulnerable populations, such as in mental health or skill development, and rights and opportunities in the job market, with service providers, who also may face issues like stress, debt, and job insecurity. There is an opportunity, then, not just to integrate residents of mixed incomes into the same housing development but also to combine support services for populations with different socio-economic background and life trajectories. The housing development or project could function as a hub for a network of initiatives and organizations, which, by acting together, may shift policy discourse and strategies away from targeting specific groups like welfare recipients or even low-income working families to confronting the state of precarity itself. Evans (2002) writes in his collection of case studies on urbanization and collective action to improve environmental sustainability:

> Each type of actor—communities, intermediary organizations, and state agencies—has a complementary contribution to make to the fight for livability. The capacity of each depends on its internal coherence as well as the aggregated experience and ability of its individual members, but the power of each to effect change also depends fundamentally on its relations to the others.
>
> (2002: 244)

The aim of transforming a field like homelessness is to develop new relationships and new dependencies while overcoming the limitations of concentrating on coherence across individual members.

Conclusion

This chapter has discussed how fields are constituted, or based on a conception of a social problem influenced in itself by policy, politics, and institutional behavior. Organizational characteristics, behavior and decision-making reflect the pressures inherent to surviving in a field, particularly if resources are scarce. Those organizations that offer alternative conceptions of the problem, and thus different types of interventions than those that predominate, can reveal how much these pressures can force consistency across the field and thus its reproduction. Likewise, fields that evolve, like legal services to assist pupils with special needs, in opposition to the government, or even other actors like private companies, can end up changing because the factors, like resources, that have maintained activism disappear or decline.

More generally, as an example of sociological analysis translated into practice, fields allow for practitioners and academics, whatever the sector or background, to interpret limitations and constraints on social change and inversely, recognize opportunities. Field analysis also recognizes that policies have implications beyond the content of services and organizations face obstacles that need articulation through a systematic framework of analysis. Developing and using this framework of analysis encourages collective reflection on how to address a social problem and importantly, how to call to account policymakers and elites often distant from the everyday experience of economic insecurity, mental illness, and so on. The conclusion discusses how concepts like a field of social action can contribute to democratic thinking and practice.

Notes

1 We are only discussing youth here.
2 Section 38 of the Crime and Disorder Act (1998). www.legislation.gov.uk/ukpga/1998/37/contents. According to the National Appropriate Adult Network (Pritchard 2006), in reality, this time is "negotiated fit with time the police wish to interview, the arrival of a legal representative, and sometimes the Forensic

Physician. Negotiated arrival times are generally beneficial both for the Appropriate Adult and the needs of the investigation" (7).

3 Pritchard (2007: 25).

4 For example, chapters of Sova run Appropriate Adult Schemes across England (Derby City, North Lincolnshire).

5 The Schemes rely more heavily on volunteers than paid Appropriate Adults for a variety of reasons, from funding to symbolic value. As the long-term volunteer put it, "Youth have more trust in volunteers."

6 The number of call-outs listed in the Service Level Agreement between the Youth Offending Team and the organization may underestimate growth. For example, the Sheffield three-year contract with Sova was for an estimated 1,000 requests for Appropriate Adults. During the fiscal year 2007–2008, the project received 1,170 call-outs (Sova Sheffield, Barnsley, and Doncaster Annual Report Appropriate Adults Scheme, p. 4).

7 Sova does offer mentoring schemes and support services for youth in prison and youth ex-offenders who have returned to their communities. However, these services do not formally overlap with the Appropriate Adult Scheme.

8 Interview with volunteer, February 15, 2009.

9 This approach can be seen in Sova annual reports, where Appropriate Adult Services are discussed in terms of number of police requests answered rather than any data about recidivism among detainees or connection to youth offending services, even the ones Sova offers.

10 According to the NAAN report (Pritchard 2006: 16), "All schemes need a minimum of one full time coordinator (or equivalent) plus some administrative and management support. This can be arranged in various ways. For example if administration and related tasks are covered within a wider organisation, this can reduce the hours necessary for a coordinator. Similarly if the rota call-outs are handled separately or other managers share the on call back up duties, this takes pressure off the coordinator's time. Rent and overheads are often not identified but absorbed in other budgets. However, all these costs need to be identified to get a true picture of the real cost of running an effective service. It is clear from the responses that these costs are often not identified. Similarly if Emergency Duty Teams pick up out of hours calls for the YOTs, these costs are not usually identified separately, but they are real costs and need to be seen as such. All of these costs take no account of in kind support, for example police assistance with training or free use of premises for training or meetings. These contributions should be seen as adding value, demonstrating how schemes bring in resources from other stakeholders."

11 http://ceo.benfredaconsulting.com/wp-content/uploads/General-Brochure-1.pdf, p. 11.

12 www.pecan.org.uk/our-history

13 www.goodwill.org/blog/my-story/pablo-gaxiola/

14 http://ceoworks.org/about/what-we-do/mission-vision/

15 https://ceoworks.org/contact-ceo-works/media-kit/

16 www.manchestercathedral.org/volunteering/volition

17 Ibid.

18 Interview with a supervisor, 1999.
19 Interview with client, 1999.
20 Interview with manager, 1999.
21 Interview with manager, 1999.
22 Interviews with supervisor and assistant manager, 1999.
23 Interview with administrator, 2000.
24 www.aje-dc.org/who-we-are/
25 www.aje-dc.org/who-we-are/
26 http://idea-b.ed.gov/explore/view/p/,root,dynamic,TopicalBrief,23,.html
27 Interview with lawyer, December 16, 2009.
28 Interview with case worker, December 17, 2009.
29 Interview with lawyer, December 16, 2009.
30 www.citizen.org/documents/Price-v-DC-Reply-and-Opposition-to-Cross-Motion.pdf and www.wrightslaw.com/idea/art/atty.fees.butler.htm
31 www.cadc.uscourts.gov/internet/opinions.nsf/0397F8EBB2B61CE7852578260055D020/$file/10-7019-1290381.pdf
32 www.cadc.uscourts.gov/internet/opinions.nsf/0397F8EBB2B61CE7852578260055D020/$file/10-7019-1290381.pdf
33 http://legaltimes.typepad.com/blt/2012/08/dc-settles-hundreds-of-attorney-fee-suits-with-special-education-law-firm.html
34 Interview with advocate, December 10, 2009.
35 Interview with former advocate, December 9, 2009.
36 DC boasts a number of mentoring programs for all age levels. A list from the volunteer organization Greater DC Cares includes 46 organizations. As the organization in question is not on it, the list is obviously incomplete. These organizations may compete for different pots of money, but the funding I have found is typically not long-term and is not substantial. For example, the Morris Cafritz Foundation offers one-year grants to programs in education for amounts typically ranging from $15,000 to $30,000. Though supportive politically of mentoring, as of Fall 2008, the George W. Bush administration had proposed a 50% cut in funding for mentoring, or a reduction from $100 million to $50 million.
37 www.bbbscapitalregion.org/site/c.evKTI6OVIpJ8H/b.8100459/k.A32F/So_many_ways_to_get_started.htm
38 Interview with director, May 11, 2005.
39 His analysis paralleled reports from other managers at mentoring organizations. One told me that he would repeatedly make appointments with school staff who would, in turn, not bother to show up.
40 HEARTH Federal Register/Vol. 76, No. 233/Monday, December 5, 2011/Rules and Regulations (75995).
41 www.dhcs.ca.gov/services/MH/Documents/ADV_2013_06_03a_HEARTH_Act_Overview.pdf
42 Interview with director, May 9, 2005.
43 www.homeaid.org/homeaid-stories/69/top-causes-of-homelessness
44 https://dchousing.org/doc.aspx?docid=57&AspxAutoDetectCookieSupport=1
45 www.community-partnership.org/facts-and-figures

46 http://some.org/wp-content/uploads/2014/08/Homelessness-More-on-the-Issue.pdf

47 In DC, the current (2016) mayor Muriel Bowser and the City Council chief policy is the construction of seven new family short-term housing facilities to replace the aging and dysfunctional DC General.

CONCLUSION

In early 2009, I conducted a series of interviews in Washington, DC with administrative staff within the local department of Health and Human Services and frontline workers in the public and nonprofit sectors. Both the administrative staff and the frontline workers, particularly those helping families with children, told me that they were seeing a dramatic uptick in applicants for benefits, from food stamps to Medicaid. One manager in the local Income Maintenance Assistance office stated that not only was he seeing more cases than ever before, he was also encountering a new population that had no experience applying for benefits and therefore did not understand the income requirements. "They felt they had paid taxes all these years and now they were getting what they were entitled to," the manager recounted (Bosman 2009: A1). Yet, when I asked a member of the city council, who happened to be a retired social worker, if he and the other council members were preparing a 'crisis' plan, he replied "No," and that he had not heard about the increase in demand.

This encounter has stayed with me, as I have interviewed numerous directors and staff members of organizations in multiple countries who feel like local and national policymakers have little awareness of the negative consequences of policy and have little interest in learning more. This book, however, is not about the specific consequences of policy, but rather how to assess current responses to problems and generate new ways of thinking, with the potential of influencing policy. George Monbiot wrote in a column for the *The Guardian*: "Persistent, determined, well-organised groups can bring neglected issues to the fore and change political outcomes. But in doing so they cannot rely on what democracy ought to be. We must see it for what it is. And that means understanding what we are" (2016). Describing 'transformative' participation in development programs, David Lewis states that ideally, those participating "find ways to make decisions and take action, without outsider involvement and on their own terms" (2014: 11). He warns, though, that "top-down interests in participation are different from bottom-up interests.... Like empowerment, participation is also a process, and people may stop participating if they do not feel their interests can be met" (118).

Appreciating Collaborative Thinking and Action

The framework outlined here of reconsidering how social problems are conceptualized and subsequently devising new, relevant social interventions and methods of organizational management hopefully represents a means of protecting bottom-up interests and changing political outcomes. Most importantly, like transformative participation, conceiving of fields of social action, in which analysis integrates identification of the problem and the response, can both overcome strategizing as individual, often competitive, organizations and encourage collective mobilization to do things differently.

Cooperation among organizations and between nonprofit organizations, business, and the government is commonplace but often not consistent or based in equality, as nonprofits often rely upon private and/or public funding. Furthermore, the public sector has–for at least several decades and increasingly all over the world–functioned as a major contractor of services both for private firms and nonprofits (Bovaird 2004; Brown et al. 2006; Ryan 2014). In contrast, considering a 'field of social action' shifts the focus from delivering a service already delineated by policy to discussing how to define the problem, the appropriate role for each sector and organization, and the relevance of specific interventions. For instance, rethinking the field of job placement services to include retention would require involving employers and potentially policymakers, who may need to encourage employer support (Sancino 2016).

However, policy has not tended to favor this kind of cooperation. Around ten years ago, I attended a meeting hosted by Voluntary Action

Conclusion

Sheffield (VAS), the local infrastructure organization responsible for providing legal, funding, and other types of support to voluntary sector organizations in Sheffield, England. VAS organized the meeting with the intention of improving relations between the Sheffield city government and the voluntary sector. It was during a period of disarray and despair in the voluntary sector, particularly for organizations working with children and young people. To become more efficient, the city government had merged education and social services. The preoccupation with reorganization within the public sector had meant delays in funding commitments to organizations running quickly out of cash and general confusion about contact between public sector agencies and charities.

After a general meeting, the organizers from VAS divided attendees into small groups to conduct an exercise in open discussion. A manager at a prominent citywide organization working with children and young people, someone I knew had been pushing for greater mobilization among voluntary sector organizations in his field, challenged the other members of the group to demonstrate coordination and strength to the public sector. "As a sector," he said, "we have never put our cards on the table, said who we are, this is what we do. We haven't done that."[1] The representative from another organization was skeptical, saying: "The problem with getting our name on the list [of representatives of the sector] is that it creates competitiveness." The manager answered quickly and firmly:

> That's what happens when the public sector leads the agenda. If we come together through the network [of organizations delivering services for youth and children], then we can get our name on the list as a sector. Then we represent whoever wants us to represent them. That means smaller organizations can participate. Before, with other bids [for public sector funds], the big organizations came in and said we have the facilities, the accreditation. It left out the small organizations.

The representative in the group from the city government concurred. She underscored the importance of mobilization among organizations and clear, logical positions on policy and funding:

> You should never underestimate your own strength. There is no way that we can deliver outcomes without you. If you don't come together though,

we will see you as small and able to be picked off. It is about understanding from the base that we have to have the same outcomes.[2]

In 2011, the director of volunteering at a local infrastructure organization in London made a similar remark about the need for small organizations to have a voice, though she was pessimistic about the government hearing, particularly after abandoning the Local Strategic Partnerships (LSPs) created under the Labour Party government to support communication between local governments and the voluntary sector. The coalition government, which came to power in 2010, cut this mandatory consultation. She stated, "Communication between the public and voluntary sectors is not as it should be because of losing LSPs." She complained that restricted communication privileged big providers of services rather than small, local organizations in bidding for contracts, despite consistent demand from the borough for community groups to be prominent in delivering social support.[3]

Lack of communication, coupled with increasing responsibility to deliver what the public sector no longer can deliver and to meet complex and growing need, has affected nonprofit organizations in other contexts as well. Describing the effects of welfare reform in the nineties on American nonprofit organizations, Reisch and Sommerfield note that the role of these organizations has become supplementary, as "nonprofit organizations fill gaps in goods and services that the government does not provide" (2003: 22). They remark, however, that, in their survey of organizations

> [T]he supplementary role did not appear to be the desired modus operandi for many of these nonprofit organizations. A general sense emerged that the public sector had abdicated much of its responsibility for the care of low-income populations to nonprofit organizations.
>
> (41)

Though the research occurred in the years after welfare reform, the sentiment and practical responsibility have arguably only become more entrenched.

At the same time, though, there are several trends encouraging collaboration and communication between actors on how to address complex and profound social problems. Mendel and Brudney (2014) look to the

Conclusion

relationships philanthropies form with charities they support as spaces "that offer the sanctuary of time, place, financial support, and expertise for participants in the partnership to work out the issues leading to meaningful partnership . . . and public value" (34). The co-production literature also pushes for partnerships, this time between local governments and business and civic society actors or between public service providers and service users. The latter process can be exclusionary, especially of minority or vulnerable groups, or for lack of resources, rely upon known local figures (Beresford 2013). However, consultation with service users has now become integrated into program design and delivery in the United Kingdom.[4]

More recent contributions to the co-production literature have concentrated on community outcomes. Actors across the three sectors, whether individuals, agencies, or businesses, each contribute to achieving particular outcomes, which together become part of a series of meta-outcomes. For instance, individual changes in behavior, in part instigated by business practices or the provision of public or nonprofit social services, contribute to larger changes in the community. The value of all of these efforts combined, as Sancino notes,

> is more than the sum of the contributions made by the parts and it is durable and sustainable, that is to say that it can be institutionalised within institutional or social structures that are part of the community, contributing to framing its identity and its social capital.
>
> (2016: 419)

The aim of an analysis of co-production of community outcomes is to understand how these outcomes are produced, through what value chains and by whom, and to what collective benefit.

The responsibility of the local government then becomes to encourage and coordinate the various actors so that they are aware of community outcomes and continue to work toward them. Sancino contends that "the strategic (re)positioning" of the local government in this direction "should aim to maximise the co-production and peer production of community outcomes, given the current roles and processes, goods, services and behaviours provided by the different actors within the community" (2016: 123). For him, "the local government becomes the pivot of different kinds of relationships and networks made up of different actors who collectively assume the responsibility for implementing an overall strategic plan of the community beyond their specific roles and interests" (2016: 123). Ideally, then, the government becomes a catalyst and a guide, generating, for supporters of co-production, a new ethos of cultivating citizenship, sustaining constructive relationships, and valuing human potential (Bovaird 2007; Verschuere et al. 2012; Pestoff 2011).

Appreciative Inquiry and Collective Impact put the principle of cooperation enabling better individual and macro-level outcomes into practice. Cooperrider et al. (2003) explain Appreciative Inquiry as using the communal development of new social theories to instigate new opportunities for dialogue and new norms and forms of social organization and action. For Cooperrider and his colleagues, social theory is a "communal creation" (2003: 344), residing in an "interactive collectivity" (2003: 344). They argue that, "Patterns of social-organizational action are not fixed by nature in any direct biological or physical way; the vast share of social conduct is potentially stimulus-free, capable of infinite conceptual variation" (2003: 343). Communities can alter organizational forms and actions through dialogue and shifts in language, creating new norms. In practice, Appreciative Inquiry means asking questions that focus on what works; for example, how an office creates a culture of trust or the kinds of feedback that make an employee feel valued (Cooperrider and Whitney 2005). One list of questions following an Appreciative Inquiry approach includes "Describe your part in a successful conclusion to a client matter you were handling. Describe an organization that you've worked in that fosters continuous learning. How has the organization done that? How do you stay energized and inspired?" The goal, then, is to determine constructive cause-and-effect relationships and replicate them in the same or other contexts.

Collective Impact, as described earlier, brings key actors together to define a common agenda and work toward common goals. A backbone organization coordinates communication between actors and provides a management structure for the overall initiative. The aim is to diminish competition and mistrust between community organizations, the public sector, and other actors, while linking areas of social action to address effectively complex problems. The latter may be quality of life in a particular neighborhood experiencing high crime rates, declining educational standards, few job opportunities, and ineffective government intervention.[5] A Collective Impact approach connects actors in each area to coordinate activities and generate a shared understanding of what needs to be done.

As models of managing local efforts to confront social problems, co-production, Appreciative Inquiry, and Collective Impact all concentrate on structural reorganization and creation of common objectives. The belief in generating new theories, or relying on the collective imagination, to expand possibilities of action in Appreciative Inquiry and the push for collectively defining a problem, namely widening the scope to include interlinked issues like hunger and joblessness in Collective Impact, acknowledge the importance of a grounded understanding of causality and needed intervention. Yet, both assume that coordinated communal efforts can achieve an understanding that in turn leads to sustained social change. In this way, they risk overreliance on the method to achieve substantive transformation. Microcredit, cooperatives, and mentoring all represent methods of instigating changes in individual behavior and attitudes, social organization (where peer relations become critical to generating income), and economic opportunities. An International Fund for Agricultural Development (IFAD) proposal for funding for the second phase of 'Livestock and Rangelands Development in the Eastern Region' in Morocco offers a stark example of the assumption that implementing a method will produce the desired results. The program aimed to "strengthen the capability of grass-roots organizations to establish a viable participatory mechanism through which the target group can drive the identification and implementation of investment opportunities" (IFAD 2003b: vi). Championing the cooperative as the appropriate "viable participatory mechanism," the proposal contends that it fits naturally as an organizational form with local kinship groups. In fact, the summary report states that, "Cooperatives are replacing traditional tribal ways as a new focus of identity and a way to deal with individual herding interests which can clash with the sustainable management of resources." The report asserts the critical position of cooperatives in transforming attitudes: "Through the cooperatives, the project has created awareness of the need to take collective action in the battle against dwindling natural resources" (2003a). The logical follow-up question is how the project created this awareness but more profoundly, is the emphasis on cooperatives as the solution the best approach or perhaps is the issue how resources are used to sustain desired livelihoods and social relations?

A conceptual framework like a 'field of social action,' which analyzes social action in a specific political economic context and critiques categorization of social problems and needs, aims first to transform the context for social intervention. This happens through shifting the basis for describing problems from measurable trends like the rate of homelessness or the number of homeless to a more qualitative understanding of the existential and material conditions homelessness produces, like vulnerability or precarity. Subsequently, rather than rethinking specific interventions and their linkages to address 'homelessness' or even—on a broader scale—local regeneration, revising a field of social action implies assigning responsibility for individual and collective potential and practical obligations to generate change. Is the state responsible for its citizens experiencing insecurity, or is it private actors or a combination? Is insecurity addressed best through the language and legal protection of rights, or do policies and specific services also have to account for other aspects of 'security' like having access to social support, which in turn, reflects organizational and institutional choices and behavior? It is by working through these questions of responsibilities and obligations, like employers supporting retention of low-skill, high-risk employees—as well as charities and the state—that services, objectives, and assessment of impact are devised.

Democracy and Social Action

The ideas presented in this book neither figure into a grand vision of political, social, and economic transformation nor provide a practical framework for evaluation. Instead, the ambition is to provide a conceptual framework that deliberately disregards barriers between social theory, research, and practice in order to provide a means—whether across organizations and policymakers as in Collective Impact or within one organization—for instigating social change. The framework of a field of social action is meant to be a tool for supporting social and ultimately political agency.

At the same time, though, reference to social and political agency evokes notions of citizenship. The politics of social action derived from reconceiving social problems and ways to address them is not the equivalent of mobilizing around a particular issue, like exploitative working conditions (Bieler and Lee 2017; Fine 2006; Das Gupta 2006). Rather, the politics of social action based on rethinking the purpose of social

Conclusion

intervention must aim for new priorities in policymaking. A new conception of a social problem—especially one that understands a problem in existential rather than material terms, such as lack of social support rather than joblessness in the Manchester organization—means that policy cannot respond by addressing particular concerns like enforcing the minimum wage or regulation of working hours. Instead, the politics of social action have to challenge policies when they limit the social imagination and collective effort. They have to expose publicly the connection between the project of building social solidarity and the process of designing, implementing, and benefiting from specific social interventions.

Political agency that looks to a process rather than a goal evokes the connection Balibar makes between citizenship and democracy (2008, 2014, 2015). He describes democracy as "a permanent struggle for its own democratization and against its own reversal into oligarchy and monopoly of power" (2008: 528). Following Rancière, he confirms that democracy is a process, or a

> permanent struggle for the democratization of its own historical institutions. It shows that there is no such thing as a consensus on democracy: actual democracy is of necessity based on conflict. It is conflictual democracy even if there must be a distinction between political conflict and civil war.
>
> (2008: 536)

The use of conceptual frameworks like a field of social action ideally allow for questioning, revising, and resisting to become constants and thus, in a way, become a means to sustain democracy. They also locate agency within a particular space and point in time, as Balibar wants in referring to democratization.

Beyond the framework, however, social action itself provides insight into how acts of citizenship constitute the struggle for democracy and how these acts reflect the particular challenges faced by activists within this struggle. For example, in an interview in 2005, the director of a center supporting carers envisioned continued expansion of government involvement in voluntary sector service provision. She commented:

> I try not to be anything other than positive. But if I were to look in ten years' time, the only way we would have grown is to meet statutory

sector targets. There is always the heavy hand of the state and it is hard to avoid it.[6]

Her prediction for small- and medium-sized organizations was dire:

> Unless the government was committed to looking at the voluntary sector completely differently and not attached to statutory sector outcomes and policies, and I can't imagine how this would happen, if they exist at all in ten years' time, there will be no small and medium-sized organization doing government work.

She believed, and she repeated this several times, that "Only church organizations, where there is fresh air and a little money, will survive. If I were to hold onto one model, it would that area, church-based organizations." A decade later, an activist in interfaith relations told me that central government cuts to their funding had forced her local council to reduce landscaping services in the local park from three times to once a month. In response, a group of residents had decided to tend to the park themselves, with the local council providing tools. "If there is one positive thing that has happened with austerity," she said, "It is that we have learned to help ourselves."[7]

Both activists were trying to protect services in a period of duress, integrating action with advocacy. Reflecting the dominant political agenda and levels of public sector spending, the first concentrated on organizational survival and the second on informal, albeit regular, activities to replace services formerly paid for by the state. For the care center director, the politics of social action had to defend the role of small- and medium-sized organizations that could offer beneficiaries intensive and flexible services whereas for the interfaith activist, this politics had to protect the capacity of individuals and groups to act to improve their quality of life. Their differences indicate margin for maneuvering and shifting ambitions at a grassroots level. At the same time, their call for public institutions and private actors to demonstrate social responsibility and to respect the right of individuals to lead a dignified life shows the importance of social action for any vision of democracy as a process. Sustaining a democracy must therefore include protecting individual activism and organizations, not just maintaining assistance for those in need but also pursuing alternative directions.

Notes

1 Interview with manager, October 19, 2006.

2 Interview with staff member, October 19, 2006.

3 Interview with director, November 21, 2014.

4 See, for example, the Social Care Institute for Excellence's guidance on co-production: www.scie.org.uk/publications/guides/guide51/recommendations.asp

5 See http://collectiveimpactforum.org/resources/featured-story-memphis-fast-forward.

6 Interview with director, November 11, 2005.

7 Interview with interfaith activist, December 12, 2016.

REFERENCES

Abu-Nimer, Mohammed. (2004) "Religion, Dialogue, and Non-Violent Actions in Palestinian-Israeli Conflict," *International Journal of Politics, Culture, and Society*, Vol. 17, No. 3 (Spring): 491–511.

Abzug, Rikki and Galaskiewicz, Joseph. (2001) "Nonprofit Boards: Crucibles of Expertise or Symbols of Local Identities?" *Nonprofit and Voluntary Sector Quarterly*, Vol. 30, No. 1 (March): 51–73. doi:7310.1177/0899764001301003

Alexander, Jennifer. (2000) "Adaptive Strategies of Nonprofit Human Service Organizations in an Era of Devolution and New Public Management," *Nonprofit Management and Leadership*, Vol. 10, No. 10: 287–303.

Aligica, Paul Dragos. (2015) "Addressing Limits to Mainstream Economic Analysis of Voluntary and Nonprofit Organizations: The 'Austrian' Alternative," *Nonprofit and Voluntary Sector Quarterly*, Vol. 44, No. 5 (October): 1026–1040.

Alzheimer's Society. (2013) "£100 Million Committed to Dementia Research in Next Decade: Alzheimer's Society Make Long-Term Funding Promise to Tackle Dementia," www.alzheimers.org.uk/site/scripts/press_article.php?pressReleaseID=1067

Audia, Pino Gaudi, Freeman, John H. and Reynolds, Paul Davidson. (2006) "Organizational Foundings in Community Context: Instruments Manufacturers and Their Interrelationship With Other Organizations," *Administrative Science Quarterly*, Vol. 51: 381–419.

Bailey, Jeffrey. (2006) "Sacred Book Club: Reading Scripture Across Interfaith Lines," *Christian Century*, Vol. 123, No. 18 (September 5). www.interfaith.cam.ac.uk/resources/scripturalreasoningresources/newmodels

Baines, Donna, Cunningham, Ian, Campey, John and Shields, John. (2014) "Not Profiting From Precarity: The Work of Nonprofit Service Delivery and the Creation of Precariousness," *Just Labour: A Canadian Journal of Work and Society*, Vol. 22 (Autumn): 74–93.

Balibar, Etienne. (2008) "Historical Dilemmas of Democracy and Their Contemporary Relevance for Citizenship," *Rethinking Marxism*, Vol. 20, No. 4: 522–538.

Balibar, Etienne. (2014) *Equaliberty: Political Essays*. Durham, NC: Duke University Press.

References

Balibar, Etienne. (2015) *Citizenship*. Cambridge, UK: Polity Press.

Bath, Chris, Bhardwa, Bina, Jacobson, Jessica, May, Tiggey and Webster, Russell. (2015) "There to Help: Ensuring Provision of Appropriate Adults for Mentally Vulnerable Adults Detained or Interviewed by Police," National Appropriate Adult Network and the Institute for Criminal Policy Research: Report for the Home Secretary, UK, August.

Baum, Joel A. C. and Oliver, Christine. (1996) "Toward an Institutional Ecology of Organizational Founding," *The Academy of Management Journal*, Vol. 39, No. 5: 1378–1427. www.jstor.org/stable/257003.

Baum, Joel A. C. and Singh, Jitendra V. (Eds.) **(**1994a) *Evolutionary Dynamics of Organizations*. Oxford: Oxford University Press.

Baum, Joel A. C. and Singh, Jitendra V. (1994b) "Organizational Hierarchies and Evolutionary Processes: Some Reflections on a Theory of Organizational Evolution," in Joel A. C. Baum and Jitendra V. Singh (eds.), *Evolutionary Dynamics of Organizations*. New York: Oxford University Press, 3–22.

Beresford, Peter. (2013) *Beyond the Usual Suspects*. London: Shaping Our Lives.

Bieler, Andreas and Lee, Chun-Yi. (2017) "Exploitation and Resistance: A Comparative Analysis of the Chinese Cheap Labour Electronics and High-Value Added IT Sectors," *Globalizations*, Vol. 14, No. 2, 202–215.

Bosman, Julie. (2009) "Newly Poor Swell Lines at Food Banks," *New York Times*, February 20, A1.

Bourdieu, Pierre. (1979) *La Distinction*. English translation (1987) *Distinction: A Social Critique of the Judgement of Taste*. Cambridge, MA: Harvard University Press. Reprint 2002.

Bourdieu, Pierre. (1987) "The Force of Law: Toward a Sociology of the Juridical Field," *The Hastings Law Journal*, Tr. Richard Terdiman, Vol. 38 (July): 805–853.

Bourdieu, Pierre and Loic Wacquant. (1992) *An Invitation to Reflexive Sociology*. Chicago: University of Chicago Press.

Bovaird, Tony. (2004) "Public-Private Partnerships: From Contested Concepts to Prevalent Practice," *International Review of Administrative Sciences*, Vol. 70, No. 2: 199–215.

Bovaird, Tony. (2007) "Beyond Engagement and Participation: User and Community Coproduction of Public Services," *Public Administration Review*, Vol. 67, Issue 5 (September-October 2007), 846–860.

Brown, Trevor, Potoski, Matthew, & Slyke, David. (2006) "Managing public service contracts: aligning values, institutions, and markets," *Public Administration Review*, 66(3): 323–332.

Bruno-van Vijfeijken, Tosca and Schmitz, Hans Peter. (2011) "A Gap Between Ambition and Effectiveness," *Journal of Civil Society*, Vol. 7, No. 3: 287–293.

Buber, Martin. (1937) *I and Thou*, transl. by Ronald Gregor Smith, Edinburgh: T. and T. Clark. 2nd ed.; New York: Scribners, 1958. 1st Scribner Classics ed.; New York: Scribner, 2000, c1986.

Burawoy, Michael. (2004) "Public Sociology: A Symposium from Boston College," *Social Problems*, Vol. 51, No. 1, 103–130.

Burawoy, Michael. (2005) "Rejoinder: Toward a Critical Public Sociology," *Critical Sociology*, Vol. 31, No. 3: 379–390.

Burawoy, Michael. (2007) "The Field of Sociology: Its Power and Its Promise," in Dan Clawson, Robert Zussman, Joya Misra, Naomi Gerstel and Randall Stokes. (eds.), *Public Sociology: Fifteen Eminent Sociologists Debate Politics and the*

References

Profession in the Twenty-First Century. Berkeley: University of California Press, 22–36.

Bushe, Gervase. (2013) "The Appreciative Inquiry Model," in Eric H. Kessler (ed.), *Encyclopedia of Management Theory*. New York: Sage. www.gervasebushe.ca/the_AI_model.pdf

Cadena-Roa, Jorge, Luna, Matilda and Puga, Cristina. (2011) "Associational Performance: The Influence of Cohesion, Decision-Making, and the Environment," *Voluntas: International Journal of Voluntary and Nonprofit Organizations*, Vol. 23, No. 4: 993–1013.

Campbell, Catherine. (2014) "Community Mobilisation in the 21st Century: Updating Our Theory of Social Change?" *Journal of Health Psychology*, Vol. 19, No. 1: 46–59. ISSN 1359-1053.

Cantwell, Wilfred. (1981) *On Understanding Islam: Selected Studies*. The Hague: Mouton.

Chapman, Hilary, Mintier, Sophie and Goodwin, Greg. (2013) "Homelessness in Metropolitan Washington: Results and Analysis from the 2013 Point-in-Time Count of Homeless Persons in the Metropolitan Washington Region," *Report Prepared by the Metropolitan Washington Council of Governments*, May 8, 2013, p. 43.

Claeyé, Frederik and Jackson, Terence. (2012) "The Iron Cage Re-Visited: Institutional Isomorphism in Non-Profit Organisations in South Africa," *Journal of International Development*, Vol. 25, No. 4: 602–622.

Cohen, Shana. (2014) "Political Identity and Social Action in Morocco," *Middle East—Topics and Arguments, Special Issue on the Middle Classes*, Vol. 2 (2014), 74–82.

Cooperrider, David L. and Whitney, Diana. (2005) *Appreciative Inquiry: A Positive Revolution in Change*. San Francisco, CA: Berrett-Koehler Publishers.

Cooperrider, David, Whitney, Diana Kaplin and Stavros, Jacqueline. (2003) *Appreciative Inquiry Handbook*. Oakland, CA: Berret-Koehler Publishers.

Das Gupta, Monisha. (2006) *Unruly Immigrants: Rights, Activism, and Transnational South Asian Politics in the United States*. Durham, NC: Duke University Press.

Davies, Rick. (2009) "An Input Into the Background Conceptual Paper: An Expanded M&E Framework for Social Change Communication," April 2009.

Davies, Siriol. (2007) *An Evaluation of Different Models of Interfaith Activity*. London: South London Inter Faith Group.

Deacon, Bob. (2007) *Global Social Policy and Governance*. London: Sage.

DiMaggio, Paul and Powell, Walter. (1983) "The Iron Cage Revisited: Institutional Isomorphism and Collective Rationality in Organizational Fields," *American Sociological Review*, Vol. 48, No. 2: 147–160.

Dimaggio, Paul J. and Powell, Walter W. (1991) "Introduction," in Paul Dimaggio and Walter Powell (eds.), *New Institutionalism in Organizational Analysis*. Chicago: University of Chicago Press.

Dwyer, Peter and Wright, Sharon. (2014) "Universal Credit, Ubiquitous Conditionality and Its Implications for Social Citizenship," *Journal of Poverty and Social Justice*, Vol. 22, No. 1 (February): 27–35(9).

Ehrenreich, Barbara. (2001) *Nickel and Dimed*. New York: Metropolitan Books.

Ellis, Jean, Parkinson, Diana and Wadia, Avan. (2011) "Making Connections: Using a Theory of Change to Develop Planning and Evaluation," www.salfordsocialvalue.org.uk/wp-content/uploads/2016/06/makingconnectionsusingatheoryofchangetodevelopplan-800-808.pdf

References

Emirbayer, Mustafa and Williams, Eva M. (2005) "Bourdieu and Social Work," *Social Service Review*, Vol. 79, No. 4 (2005): 689–724. doi:10.1086/491604

Evans, Peter. (2002) "Political Strategies for More Livable Cities: Lessons from Six Cases of Development and Political Transition," in Peter Evans (ed.), *Urban Struggles for Livelihood and Sustainability*. Berkeley: University of California Press, 222–246.

Everly, George S. (2011) "Building a Resilient Organizational Culture," *Harvard Business Review*, June 24.

Fine, Janice. (2006) *Worker Centers: Organizing Communities at the Edge of a Dream*. Ithaca, NY: Cornell University ILR School.

Fitzpatrick, Jody L. (2012) "An Introduction to Context and Its Role in Evaluation Practice," *New Directions for Evaluation*, Vol. 2012, No. 135 (Fall), 7–24. doi:10.1002/ev.20024

Fitzpatrick, Jody, Sanders, James and Worthen, Blaine. (2004) *Program Evaluation—Alternative Approaches and Practical Guidelines*. 3rd ed. New York: Allyn and Bacon.

Galaskiewicz, Joseph. (1997) "An Urban Grants Economy Revisited: Corporate Charitable Contributions in the Twin Cities, 1979–1981, 1987–1989," *Administrative Science Quarterly*, Vol. 42: 445–471.

Gamble, Jamie. (2008) *A Developmental Evaluation Primer*. Montreal: The J.W. McConnell Family Foundation.

Garfinkel, Renee. (2004) *What Works? Evaluating Interfaith Dialogue Programs*. Washington, DC: United States Institute of Peace.

Garringer, Michael, Kupersmidt, Janis, Rhodes, Jean, Stelter, Rebecca and Tai, Tammy. (2015) *Elements of Effective Practice for Mentoring* (4th ed.), Boston: Mentor.

Gilbert, Jeremy. (2014) "Common Ground," *Open Democracy*, June 18. www.opendemocracy.net/ourkingdom/jeremy-gilbert/common-ground

Green, Maia. (2014) *The Development State: Aid, Culture and Civil Society in Tanzania* (African Issues). Woodbridge, UK: James Currey.

Green, Maia and Mosse, David. (Ed.) (2011) "Calculating Compassion: Accounting for Categorical Practices in International Development," in David Mosse (ed.), *Adventures in Aidland: The Anthropology of Professionals in International Development*. London: Berghahn, 33–58.E

Greene, J. C. (2005) "Context," in Sandra Matheson (ed.), *Encyclopedia of Evaluation*. Thousand Oaks, CA: Sage, 82–84.

Guo, Chao and Brown, William A. (2006) "Community Foundation Performance: Bridging Community Resources and Needs," *Nonprofit and Voluntary Sector Quarterly*, Vol. 35, No. 2: 267–287.

Hansard, The. (2014, November 27) "Religion and Belief: British Public Life," Motion to Take Note, 11.53 am, Moved by Lord Harries of Pentregarth, 12.33 pm (Lord Parekh), Column 1015.

Hardt, Michael and Negri, Antonio. (2000) *Empire*. Cambridge, MA: Harvard University Press.

Hatak, Isabella; Lang, Richard; and Roessl, Deitmar. (2016) "Trust, Social Capital, and the Coordination of Relationships Between the Members of Cooperatives: A Comparison Between Member-Focused Cooperatives and Third-Party-Focused Cooperatives," *Voluntas: International Journal of Voluntary and Nonprofit Organizations*, Vol. 27: 1218–1241.

Hickey, Sam and Mohan, Giles (eds.). (2004) "Towards Participation as Transformation: Critical Themes and Challenges for a Post-Tyranny Agenda," in *Participation: From Tyranny to Transformation? Exploring New Approaches to Particpation in Development*. London: Zed Books, 3–24.

Hickey, Sam and Mohan, Giles. (2005) "Relocating Participation Within a Radical Politics of Development," *Development and Change*, Vol. 36, No. 2: 237–262. doi:10.1111/j.0012-155X.2005.00410.x

Hwang, Hokyu and Powell, Walter W. (2009) "The Rationalization of Charity: The Influences of Professionalism in the Nonprofit Sector," *Administrative Science Quarterly*, Vol. 54, No. 2 (June): 268–298.

Individuals with Disabilities Education Improvement Act, 20 U.S.C. §1400 (2004).

International Fund for Agricultural Development. (2003a) "Managing the 'Commons': Livestock and Pasture Development Project in the Eastern Region," Evaluation Profile, No. 11, April, www.ifad.org/evaluation/reports/profile/tags/land/morocco/260/y2003/2586436

International Fund for Agricultural Development. (2003b) "Report and Recommendation of the President to the Executive Board on a Proposed Loan to the Kingdom of Morocco for the Livestock and Rangelands Development Project in the Eastern Region – Phase II," Rome: IFAD, September 10-11, https://www.ifad.org/documents/10180/d40d96c7-65e1-4586-870c-67dab1bf7a46

Joseph, Mark L. (2006) "Creating Mixed-Income Developments in Chicago: Developer and Service Provider Perspectives," *Housing Policy Debate*, Vol. 20, No. 1: 91–118. doi:10.1080/10511481003599894

Joseph, Mark L., LaFrance, Steven, Latham, Nancy and Kleit, Rachel Garshick. (2015) "*Can San Francisco Get Mixed-Income Housing Right?*" *Shelterforce On-Line*, December 8. Montclair, NJ: National Housing Institute. www.shelterforce.org/article/4329/can_san_francisco_get_mixed-income_public_housing_redevelopment_right/

Kamat, Sangeeta. (2004) "The Privatization of Public Interest: Theorizing NGO Discourse in Neoliberal Era," *Review of International Political Economy*, Vol. 11, No. 1: 155–176.

Kania, John and Kramer, Mark. (2011) "Collective Impact," *Stanford Social Innovation Review*, Winter. https://ssir.org/articles/entry/collective_impact

Katz, Michael. (1995) *Improving Poor People: The Welfare State, the "Underclass," and Urban Schools as History*. Princeton, NJ: Princeton University Press.

Kettner, Peter, Maroney, Peter and Martin, Lawrence. (2008) *Designing and Managing Programs: An Effectiveness-Based Approach*. 3rd ed. Thousand Oaks, CA: Sage.

Kitwood, Tom. (1993) "Towards a Theory of Dementia Care: The Inter-Personal Process," *Ageing and Society*, Vol. 13: 51–67.

Kitwood, Tom. (1997) *Dementia Reconsidered: The Person Comes First*. Buckingham, UK: Open University Press.

Lazar, Sian. (2012) "Citizenship Quality: A New Agenda for Development?" *Journal of Civil Society*, Vol. 8, No. 4: 333–350.

Leiter, Jeffrey. (2005) "Structural Isomorphism in Australian Nonprofit Organizations," *Voluntas: International Journal of Voluntary and Nonprofit Organizations*, Vol. 16: 1. doi:10.1007/s11266-005-3230-1

Leiter, J. (2013) "An Industry Fields Approach to Isomorphism Involving Australian Nonprofit Organizations," *Voluntas: International Journal of Voluntary and Nonprofit Organizations*, Vol. 24, No. 4: 1037–1070, www.jstor.org/stable/42629855

Levinas, Emmanuel. (1990) *Difficult Freedom: Essays on Judaism*. Baltimore: Johns Hopkins University Press.

References

Lewis, David. (2014) *Non-Governmental Organizations, Management and Development*. London: Routledge.

Li, Tania Murray. (2007) *The Will to Improve: Governmentality, Development, and the Practice of Politics*. Durham, NC: Duke University Press.

Liebling, Alison. (2015) "Appreciative Inquiry, Generative Theory, and the 'Failed State' Prison,'" in J. Miller and W. Palacios (eds.), *Advances in Criminological Theory*. Piscataway, NJ: Transaction Publishers, 251–270.

Liebling, Alison; Pierce, David; and Elliott, Charles. (1999) "Appreciative Inquiry and Relationships in Prison," *Punishment and Society: The International Journal of Penology*, Vol. 1, No. 1: 71–98.

Light, Paul. (2003) "The Health of the Human Services Workforce," Washington, DC: Brookings Institution.

Lincoln, James R. and Miller, Jon. (1979) "Work and Friendship Ties in Organizations: A Comparative Analysis of Relation Networks," *Administrative Science Quarterly*, Vol. 24, No. 2 (June): 181–199.

Lopez, M. Elena. (2005) "A Conversation With Jennifer Greene," *The Evaluation Exchange*, Vol. XI, No. 3 (Fall): 3–4.

Luengo-Fernandez, Ramon, Leal, Jose, and Gray, Alistair. (2015) "UK Research Spend in 2008 and 2012: Comparing Stroke, Cancer, Coronary Heart Disease and Dementia," *British Medical Journal Open* Vol. 5 (April): e006648. doi:10.1136/bmjopen-2014-006648

Lynn, Jenny (2008) "Community Leadership Approaches to Tackling Street Crime," *Joseph Rowntree Foundation*, May 15.

Mannell, Jenevieve (2012) "'It's Just Been Such a Horrible Experience,' Perceptions of Gender Mainstreaming by Practitioners in South African Organisations," *Gender & Development*, Vol. 20, No. 3: 423–434. doi:10.1080/13552074.2012.731753

Marquis, Christopher and Battilana, Julie. (2009) "Acting Globally But Thinking Locally? The Influence of Local Communities on Organizations," *Research in Organizational Behavior*, Vol. 29: 283–302.

Marquis, Christopher, Glynn, Mary Ann and Davis, Gerald(2007) "Community Isomorphism and Corporate Social Action," *Academy of Management Review*, Vol. 32, No. 3: 925–945.

Marquis, Christopher and Huang, Zhi. (2010) "Acquisitions as Exaptation: The Legacy of Founding Institutions in the U.S. Commercial Banking Industry," *Academy of Management Journal*, Vol. 53, No. 6: 1441–1473.

Marquis, Christopher and Tilcsik, Andras. (2013) "Imprinting: Toward a Multilevel Theory," *Academy of Management Annals*, Vol. 7, No. 1 (2013): 195–245.

Mendel, S. C. and Brudney, Jeffrey (2014) "Doing Good, Public Good, and Public Value," *Nonprofit Management and Leadership*, Vol. 25: 23–40. doi:10.1002/nml.21109

Meyer, John W. and Rowan, Brian. (1977) "Institutionalized Organizations: Formal Structure as Myth and Ceremony," *American Journal of Sociology*, Vol. 83, No. 2 (September): 340–363.

Mitchell, Gary and Agnelli, Joanne. (2015) "Person-Centred Care for People With Dementia: Kitwood Reconsidered," *Nursing Standard*, Vol. 30, No. 7: 46–50.

Monbiot, George. (2016) "Lies, Fearmongering, and Fables: That's Our Democracy," *The Guardian*, October 4.

Neufeldt, Reina C. (2011) "Interfaith Dialogue: Assessing Theories of Change," *Peace & Change*, Vol. 36, No. 3: 344–345.

Newman, Ines. (2008) "Work as a Route Out of Poverty," *Policy Studies*, Vol. 32, No. 2: 91–108.

O'Connor, Alice. (2001) *Poverty Knowledge: Social Science, Social Policy, and the Poor in Twentieth-Century U.S. History*. Princeton, NJ: Princeton University Press.

Oliver, Christine. (1991) "Strategic Responses to Institutional Processes," *The Academy of Management Review*, Vol. 16, No. 1 (1991): 145–179.

Oxfam. (2009) "Blind Optimism: Challenging the Myths about Private Health Care in Developing Countries," *Oxfam Briefing Paper*, February 2009.

Patterson, Orlando. (2007) "About Public Sociology," in Dan Clawson, Robert Zussman, Joya Misra, Naomi Gerstel and Randall Stokes (eds.). *Public Sociology: Fifteen Eminent Sociologists Debate Politics and the Profession in the Twenty-First Century*. Berkeley: University of California Press, 176–194

Patton, Michael Quinn. (1994) "Developmental Evaluation," *Evaluation Practice*, Vol. 15, No. 3: 311–320.

Patton, Michael Quinn. (2010) *Development Evaluation: Applying Complexity Concepts to Enhance Innovation and Use*. New York: Guildford Press.

Pedrini, Matteo, Bramanti, Valentina, Ferri, Laura Maria and Minciullo, Marco. (2016) "The Role of Social Capital in the Start-Up of Non-Profit Organisations: The Case of Fondazione Welfare Ambrosiano," *Voluntas: International Journal of Voluntary and Nonprofit Organizations*, Vol. 27, No. 3: 1195–1217.

Perlmutter, Felice, Deckop, John, Konrad, Alison and Freely, Joshua. (2005) "Nonprofits and the Job Retention of Former Welfare Clients," *Nonprofit and Voluntary Sector Quarterly*, Vol. 34, No. 4.

Pestoff, Victor. (2011) "Co-production and Third Sector Social Services in Europe—Some Crucial Conceptual Issues," in V. Pestoff, T. Brandsen, and B. Verschuere (eds.), *New Public Governance, the Third Sector and Co-Production*. London: Routledge, 13–34.

Petras, James. (1999) "NGOs: In the Service of Imperialism," *Journal of Contemporary Asia*, Vol. 29, No. 4: 429–440.

Pike, Matthew. (2014) *Mass Collaboration: How We Can Transform the Impact of Public Funding*. London: Institute of Public Policy Research.

Pritchard, Elisabeth. (2006) "Appropriate Adult Provision in England and Wales," *National Appropriate Adult Network Report Prepared for the Home Office*.

Pritchard, Elisabeth. (2007) "Appropriate Adults in the Youth Justice System," *Report for the National Association of Appropriate Adults*.

Ramanath, Ramya. (2009) "Limits to Institutional Isomorphism: Examining Internal Institutional Processes in NGO-Government Interactions," *Nonprofit and Voluntary Sector Quarterly*, Vol. 38, No. 1: 51–76.

Rand, Graham. (2000) "Critical Chain: The Theory of Constraints Applied to Project Management," *International Journal of Project Management*, Vol. 18: 173–177.

Ravallion, Martin. (2008) "Evaluating Anti-Poverty Programs," *Handbook of Development Economics*, Volume 4: 3788–3846.

Reisch, Michael and Sommerfeld, David. (2003) "Welfare Reform and the Future of Nonprofit Organizations," *Nonprofit Management and Leadership*, Vol. 14: 19–46. doi:10.1002/nml.19

Roberts, Celia, Cooke, Melanie, Baynham, Mike and Simpson, James. (2007) "Adult ESOL in the United Kingdom: Policy and Research," *Prospect*, Vol. 22, No. 3: 18–31.

References

Rog, Debra. (2012) "When Background Becomes Foreground: Toward Context-Sensitive Evaluation Practice," in D. J. Rog, J. L. Fitzpatrick, and R. F. Conner (eds.), *Context: A Framework for Its Influence on Evaluation Practice: New Directions for Evaluation*, 135. 25–40.

Rosenvallon, Pierre. (2013) *A Society of Equals*. Cambridge, MA: Harvard University Press.

Roy, Michael, Katsunori, Sato and Calò, Francesca. (2015) "Further Limits to Institutional Isomorphism? Introducing the 'Neo-Contingency Approach' to the Field of Community Led Social Ventures," *Voluntas: International Journal of Voluntary and Nonprofit Organizations*, Vol. 26, No. 6: 2536–2553. doi:10.1007/s11266-014-9529-z

Runnymede Trust. (2012) "First Report of Session 2012-13, All Party Parliamentary Group on Race and Community Ethnic Minority Female Unemployment: Black, Pakistani and Bangladeshi Heritage Women," London: Runnymede Trust.

Ryan, Laird (2014) "Outsourcing and the Voluntary Sector," National Coalition for Independent Action, *Working Paper 5*.

Sancino, Alessandro. (2016) "The Meta Co-Production of Community Outcomes: Towards a Citizens' Capabilities Approach," *Voluntas: International Journal of Voluntary Nonprofit Organizations*, Vol. 27, No. 1 (February): 409–424.

Scriven, Michael. (2016) "Roadblocks to Recognition and Revolution," *American Journal of Evaluation*, Vol. 37, No. 1: 27–44.

Smith, Victoria and Halpin, Brian. (2014) "Low-Wage Work Uncertainty Often Traps Low-Wage Workers," *UC Davis Center for Poverty Research Policy Brief*.

Standing, Guy. (2011) *The Precariat: The New Dangerous Class*. London and New York: Bloomsbury Academic.

Standing, Guy. (2014) *A Precariat Charter: From Denizens to Citizens*. London and New York: Bloomsbury Academic.

Steane, Peter and Christie, Michael. (2001) "Nonprofit Boards in Australia: A Distinctive Governance Approach," *Corporate Governance: An International Review*, Vol. 9: 48–58. doi:10.1111/1467-8683.00225

Swartz, David. (1996) "Bridging the Study of Culture and Religion: Pierre Bourdieu's Political Economy of Symbolic Power," *Sociology of Religion*, Vol. 57, No. 1: 71–85.

Tendler, Judith and Freedheim, Sarah. (1994) "Trust in a Rent-Seeking World: Health and Government Transformed in Northeast Brazil," *World Development*, Vol. 22, No. 12: 1771–1791.

Thorley, Sarah. (2007) *Improved Understanding of South London's Multi-Faith Situation*. London: South London Interfaith Group.

Tierney, Joseph P., Grossman, Jean Baldwin and Resch, Nancy. (2000) *Making a Difference: An Impact Study of Big Brothers Big Sisters*. Philadelphia: Public & Private Ventures.

Twombly, Eric. (2003) "What Factors Affect the Entry and Exit of Nonprofit Human Service Organizations in Metropolitan Areas?" *Nonprofit and Voluntary Sector Quarterly*, Vol. 32, No. 2 (June): 211–235. doi:10.1177/0899764003032002003

Unger, Roberto. (2014) *The Religion of the Future*. Cambridge, MA: Harvard University Press.

Vacca, Richard. (2007) "The Winkelman Case: Pro Se Parents in Court," *CEPI Education Law Newsletter*, March 2007, Vol. 5–7.

Vermeulen, Floris, Minkoff, Debra and van der Meer, Tom. (2014) "The Local Embedding of Community-Based Organizations," *Nonprofit and Voluntary Sector Quarterly*, Vol 45, Issue 1, pp. 23–44.

Verschuere, Bram, Brandsen, Taco and Pestoff, Victor. (2012) "Co-Production: The State of the Art in Research and the Future Agenda," *Voluntas: International Journal of Voluntary and Nonprofit Organizations*, Vol. 20, No. 1: 1–19.

Vollmer, Hendrik. (2013) *The Sociology of Disruption, Disaster, and Social Change*. Cambridge, UK: Cambridge University Press.

W. W. Kellogg Foundation. (1998) *W. W. Kellogg Foundation Evaluation Handbook*. (Updated January 2004).

Watts, Ben, Fitzpatrick, Suzanne, Bramley, Glen and Watkins, Glen. (2014) "Welfare Sanction and Conditionality in the UK," *Joseph Rowntree Foundation*, September 2014.

Webster, David. (2013) "The DWP's Updated Statistics on JSA Sanctions: What Do They Show? Further Supplementary Evidence Submitted to the Inquiry Into the Role of Jobcentre Plus in the Reformed Welfare System," November 20. www.welfareconditionality.ac.uk/wp-content/ uploads/2013/12/HofC-WPC-DW-Suppl-Evidence-2-20-Nov-2013.pdf

Weiss, Carol. (1998) "Theory-Based Evaluation: Past, Present, and Future," *American Journal of Evaluation*, Vol. 1997, No. 76 (Winter): 41–55.

Whitehead, Tom. (2008) "Immigration Is Out of Control," *Daily Express*, June 2.

Wilson, William Julius. (1996) *When Work Disappears: The World of the New Urban Poor*. New York: Knopf.

World Bank. (2002) "Morocco—Alpha Maroc Project," Washington, DC: World Bank, http://documents.worldbank.org/curated/en/428971468758091413/Morocco-Alpha-Maroc-Project

World Bank. (2008) "Morocco—Alpha Maroc Project," Washington, DC: World Bank, http://documents.worldbank.org/curated/en/321061468274747714/Morocco-Alpha-Maroc-Project

Wright, Gemma and Noble, Michael. (2012) "Does Widespread Lack Undermine the Socially Perceived Necessities Approach to Defining Poverty? Evidence From South Africa," *Journal of Social Policy*, Vol. 42, No. 1: 147–165. Published online August 29, 2012. doi:10.1017/S0047279412000530

Young, Denis. (2000) "Alternative Models of Government-Nonprofit Sector Relations: Theoretical and International Perspectives," *Nonprofit and Voluntary Sector Quarterly*, Vol. 29, No. 1: 149–172.

Zucker, Lynne. (1987) "Institutional Theories of Organization," *Annual Review of Sociology*, Vol. 13 (August): 443–464. doi:10.1146/annurev.so.13.080187.002303

Zussman, Robert and Misra, Joya. (2007) "Introduction," in Dan Clawson, Robert Zussman, Joya Misra, Naomi Gerstel, Randall Stokes and Douglas L. Anderton (eds.), *Public Sociology: Fifteen Eminent Sociologists Debate Politics and the Profession in the Twenty-First Century*. Berkeley: University of California Press, 3–22.

INDEX

Advocates for Justice and Education 102
Age Concern 72, 79n22
Aid for Families with Dependent Children (AFDC) 58
Alpha Maroc Project 12
Alzheimer's Society 76
analysis of social action *see* evaluation or analysis of social action
Appreciative Inquiry (AI) 69, 124–5
Appropriate Adult Service 81
Appropriate Adults Scheme 48–53, 55–6, 59, 80–2, 98, 115n2, 116nn4–10
Ariadne de Rothschild Fellowships 30
AT&T 5

Barnardos 77n2
ben Barka, Mehdi 10
Big Brothers, Big Sisters 104
Birmingham Faith Forum 36
British Council 32
Buber, Martin 28–9, 41
Burawoy, Michael 23–4, 45n34

Cambridge Interfaith Programme (CIP) 32–3
Campbell, Catherine 22–3
Cantwell, Wilfred 28
Center for Employment Opportunities (CEO) 89–90, 91, 92, 93
Charities Evaluation Services 11
Child Funeral Charity 6
children and adolescents: frontline initiatives working with disabled 9–10; funeral cost support services related to 6; girls' school attendance/toilet provision for 18, 45n30; mentoring programs for 54, 60, 103–8, 117n36; pediatric care initiatives for 8–9; special needs educational advocacy for 98–102; youth offender assistance programs for 48–53, 55–6, 59, 62–8, 80–2, 98, 115n2, 116nn4–10
Chinese Health Living Centre 11
Church of England: job placement services 91–2; Lambeth Jewish Forum 29
Church Urban Fund 36, 65
Citizens' Advice Bureau (CAB) 56, 61, 78n7
citizenship 12–13, 14, 16, 37, 43, 112, 124, 126–7
City of London 32
Coexist 30, 32–3
collaborative thinking and action 120–6
Collective Impact initiatives 16–17, 58, 124–5
community mobilization 22–3, 37–9, 128
Community Partnership 110–11
context of social action: Appreciative Inquiry evaluating 69; bureaucracy in 65; constraints in 55, 56–68; definition of 27; Developmental Evaluation of 69–70; embeddedness in 57; evaluation or analysis impacted by 26, 27–8, 45n37, 54, 55–6, 58–9, 67–70, 83; funding in relation to 55, 56, 58, 61, 66, 75–6; imprinting of 57; needs for

139

service in 53–4, 56, 73; opportunities for increased service and effectiveness in 55, 68–76; organizational capacity in 55, 57, 61; organizational survival and innovation in 57, 58, 62–4, 70–1, 77; overview of 3–4, 76–7; personal dislike or animosity in 65–6, 68; person-centered approach in 73–6; policy influencing 51, 55, 61, 74; politics influencing 55, 71; project management and 48–53, 71–2; resilience capacity in 69; rethinking social interventions in light of 53–76; sanctions reducing benefits in 61–2; social network analysis of 58–61; social networks influencing 49, 50, 51–2, 58–61, 68, 72–5; socioeconomic divide in 63–5, 66–7; training of volunteers in 49, 50, 52; trust of participants in 71–2
Cooperrider, David 69
Council of Christians and Jews 32
Crawley Interfaith Network 31
Crime and Disorder Act of 1998 80–1

dementia care, context for 73–6
Dementia Research Institute 76
democracy, social action and 42–3, 120, 126–8
Department for Communities and Local Government (UK) 31
Department for Investment, Universities, and Skills (UK) 13
Department of Homeless Services (UK) 87–8
Department of Works and Pensions (UK) 6
Developmental Evaluation 69–70
Dinham, Adam 35–6
disabilities, persons with: context for social action with 61–2; frontline initiatives working with 9–10; special needs educational advocacy for 98–102
Down to Earth 6

East of England Faiths Council 32
economic status *see* poverty and economic insecurity; socioeconomic status
educational social action: girls' school attendance/toilet provision as 18, 45n30; high school success initiatives as 4–5; literacy initiatives as 5, 9, 11–16, 28, 30–1, 32–3, 41, 54; mentoring programs as 54, 60, 103–8, 117n36; research informing teaching 23–4;

special needs educational advocacy programs as 98–102
embeddedness 15, 22, 57, 89
evaluation or analysis of social action: altering fields of social action based on 108–15; Appreciative Inquiry for 69, 124, 125; Collective Impact as 16–17, 58, 124–5; comparative evaluation framework for 26, 28; context significance for 26, 27–8, 45n37, 54, 55–6, 58–9, 67–70, 83; Developmental Evaluation for 69–70; diversity and commonality in interventions in 6, 33–4, 84, 85–97; faith-based and interfaith 25–42; 'field' determination for 84–8; funding in relation to 5, 27, 31–3, 82, 86, 87, 100, 103, 107–8, 113; of homelessness initiatives 87–8, 109–15; of job placement services 89–97; of mentoring programs 103–8, 117n36; organizational service changes reflecting 103–8; organizational survival and innovation in relation to 84, 86–8; overview of 4–6, 115; policy and politics in relation to 16, 25–6, 35, 37–42, 80–1, 83, 84, 89, 92, 97, 98–9, 101, 103, 108, 109–13, 117n36; project design-expected impact framework for 26, 83–108; public sector-organization relationships in 97–102, 103–4, 106–8; questioning social problem conception in 88–97, 109, 113–14; questions to ask for 84; randomized selection method of 26; replication of successful project reflecting 98; research reflecting 17, 26, 34, 82–3, 92, 93, 103, 109; resilience capacity approach for 69; shared methods of intervention in 5–6, 84; social network analysis as 58–61, 83; social network importance to 83, 86–7, 92–3, 97, 102; of special needs educational advocacy programs 98–102; theory-based 10–11, 24–5, 108–9; Theory of Change approach to 10–11, 36, 44n20, 54, 91; transformation of organizations reflecting 84, 103–15; trust and respect elements of 83–4, 93–7, 112–13; of youth offender assistance program 80–2, 98, 115n2, 116nn4–10
Every Student Succeeds Act 99

140

Index

faith-based and interfaith social action: community mobilization for 37–9, 128; engagement in 40–2; evaluation or analysis of 25–42; failure of evaluation of 25; funding for 31–3, 35, 36, 103; job placement services as 91, 92, 96–7; leadership of 31, 35–6, 42; mentoring programs as 103–8; neutral forums for 28–42; policy in relation to 1, 35, 37, 40–2; politics in relation to 35, 37–40; radicalism lack in 39–40; religious literacy initiatives as 28, 30–1, 32–3, 41; scriptural reasoning as 30–1, 32; social networks impacting 19, 31, 32, 35, 39, 59; survival of 128; transformation of theory into 40–2; *see also* specific faith-based organizations
Faith-based Regeneration Network 31
Faiths Forum For London 29, 33
'Family Engagement for High School Success' initiative 5
Fethullah Gulen Rumi Forum 29
fields of social action: collaborative thinking and action on 120–6; context for (*see* context of social action); definition of field for 2–3; democracy and 42–3, 120, 126–8; evaluation or analysis of (*see* evaluation or analysis of social action); funding for (*see* funding); policy impacting (*see* policy); politics impacting (*see* politics); research on (*see* research)
funding: collaborative thinking and action in relation to 120–3; context of social action in relation to 55, 56, 58, 61, 66, 75–6; evaluation or analysis in relation to 5, 27, 31–3, 82, 86, 87, 100, 103, 107–8, 113; for faith-based and interfaith social action 31–3, 35, 36, 103; organizational capacity impacted by 55; policy and policymakers impacting 1–2, 12–15; politics of 19–20; research on practice of 20–2; social networks impacting 15, 19–20, 21
funeral cost support services 6

gender mainstreaming 7–8
Global Family Research Project 5
Global Fund 21
Goodwill 89–90, 92, 93

Handicap International 9
Harvard Family Research Project 5
HEARTH Act 109–10, 111–12

Home Aid America 110
homelessness initiatives 6, 87–8, 109–15
hunger and food scarcity 44n20, 61–2
Hunger Project 44n20

imprinting 57
Individuals with Disabilities Education Act 99
Individuals with Disabilities Improved Education Act 99, 101
Interfaith Network 25, 29, 31, 32
interfaith social action *see* faith-based and interfaith social action
Interfaith Week 25
International Fund for Agricultural Development (IFAD) 125
isomorphism 85–6; coercive 85; mimetic 85; normative 85
Israel, public sector-nonprofit relationships in 98

Japan, public sector-nonprofit relationships in 98
job placement services 89–97, 120

Kellogg Foundation 58
King's Fund 11

Lammy, David 16
Learning and Skills Council (LSC) 15
Leicestershire County Council 33
Leicestershire Interfaith Forum 33
literacy initiatives: British 12–16; Moroccan 5, 9, 11–12, 13–14, 15–16; needs underlying 54; religious 28, 30–1, 32–3, 41
London Boroughs Faiths Network 29, 33

mass collaboration initiatives 16
McKinney-Vento Homeless Assistance Act 109
Mentor 54
mentoring programs 54, 60, 103–8, 117n36
Millennium Development Goals 4, 5
Ministry of Agriculture (Moroccan) 18
Morocco: agricultural cooperatives 18, 125; girls' school attendance/toilet provision in 18, 45n30; literacy initiatives in 5, 9, 11–12, 13–14, 15–16; pediatric care initiatives in 8–9; tuberculosis initiatives in 21–2

141

INDEX

Morris Cafritz Foundation 117n36
Muslim-Jewish Forum (Manchester, UK) 29–30, 33

National Health Service 6, 73–5
National Network of Appropriate Adults 82
Near Neighbours Programme 30, 36–7
needs, context reflecting 53–4, 56, 73
neo-institutionalism 85, 89
neoliberalism 17, 23
No Child Left Behind 99
nongovernmental organizations (NGOs): disabled children initiatives by 9–10; literacy initiatives of 9, 12, 13–14; pediatric care initiatives of 8–9

organizations *see* practitioners

Partners in Health Programme 11
Patton, Michael Quincy 69–70
Pecan 90, 92
Police and Criminal Evidence Act of 1984 80
policy: collaborative thinking and action in relation to 120–6; community mobilization integration with 22–3; context of social action influenced by 51, 55, 61, 74; cross-national policy agendas 25; democracy and 42–3, 120, 126–8; evaluation of social action in relation to 16, 25–6, 35, 37, 40–2, 80–1, 84, 92, 97, 98–9, 101, 109–13, 117n36; faith-based and interfaith social action in relation to 1, 35, 37, 40–2; funding outcomes reflecting 1–2, 12–15; overview of impacts of 1–3; political goals translated into 12–14, 15–16; practitioner criticism of 7–9, 14–16; practitioner impacts of 12–16, 119; research on impacts of 2, 17–24; social networks influencing 19, 83
politics: community mobilization integration with 22–3; context of social action influenced by 55, 71; democracy and 42–3, 120, 126–8; evaluation of social action in relation to 16, 35, 37–9, 83, 89, 92, 98, 103, 108, 117n36; faith-based and interfaith social action impacted by 35, 37–9; frontline work *vs.* 9–10; funding and 19–20; policy development from 12–14, 15–16; practitioner impacts of 11–14, 15–16
poverty and economic insecurity: context for 56, 61–2, 64–8; funeral cost issues

due to 6; job placement services impacting 89–97, 120; social problems underlying 91–2; of tuberculosis patients 22; *see also* homelessness initiatives; hunger and food scarcity
practitioners: collaborative thinking and action among 120–6; context of social action for (*see* context of social action); evaluation of (*see* evaluation or analysis of social action); faith-based (*see* faith-based and interfaith social action); frontline work of 9–10; organizational capacity of 55, 57, 61; organizational survival and innovation of 57–8, 62–4, 70–1, 77, 84, 86–8, 128; policy and politics impacts on 11–16, 119 (*see also* policy; politics); policy criticisms by 7–9, 14–16; project management by 48–53, 71–2; public sector relationships with 97–102, 103–4, 106–8, 121–6; resilience capacity of 69; social networks with (*see* social networks); *see also* specific organizations
project management 48–53, 71–2
public sociology 23–4, 45n34

Quaker Social Action 6

Regeneration Team 64–8
religious literacy initiatives 28, 30–1, 32–3, 41; *see also* faith-based and interfaith social action
research: ethnographic 20, 82–3; evaluation or analysis of social action reflected in 17, 26, 34, 82–3, 92, 93, 103, 109; on policy impacts 2, 17–24; on social networks 19–22; teaching informed by 23–4
resilience, capacity for 69
Resilience Research Centre 69
Richmond Interfaith Forum 29

scriptural reasoning 30–1, 32
Sheffield City Council 73
Sheffield Health and Social Care Trust 73–4
Shelter 6
Sikh forum 36
social action *see* fields of social action
social networks: context of social action influenced by 49, 50, 51–2, 58–61, 68, 72–5; evaluation or analysis of social

142

Index

action in relation to 83, 86–7, 92–3, 97, 102; in faith-based and interfaith social action 19, 31–2, 35, 39, 59; funding based on 15, 19–20, 21; research on 19–22; social network analysis of 58–61, 83

socioeconomic status, context reflecting 63–5, 66–7; *see also* poverty and economic insecurity

So Others May Eat (SOME) 111–12

South Africa, gender mainstreaming in 7–8

Sova 77n3, 81–2, 116n4, 116nn6–7, 116n9

special needs educational advocacy programs 98–102

Stayput 72

Sustainable Development Goals 4

Teach for America 100

Theory of Change (ToC) 10–11, 36, 44n20, 54, 91

Theory of Constraints 56–7

3FF (Three Faiths Forum) 30, 31–3, 34

transformative participation 120

trust and respect of participants: in context of social action 71–2; evaluation or analysis of social action in terms of 83–4, 93–7, 112–13

United Kingdom: charities evaluation organization in 11; collaborative thinking and action in 120–3; context of social action in 48–53, 55–6, 59–68, 71–6; dementia care in 73–6; evaluation or analysis of social action in 80–2, 90–7, 98, 109, 115n2, 116nn4–10; faith-based and interfaith social projects in 1, 25–42, 59; funeral cost reduction support services in 6; homeless and housing advocacy in 6, 109; job placement services in 90–7; literacy initiatives in 12–16; public sector-nonprofit relationships in 98, 121–3; youth offender assistance program in 48–53, 55–6, 59, 62–8, 80–2, 98, 115n2, 116nn4–10

United Nations Development Program (UNDP) 5

United States: context for social action in 56, 58, 60; evaluation or analysis of social action in 27, 89–115, 117n36; high school success initiatives in 4–5; homelessness/transitional housing initiatives in 109–15; job placement services in 89–97; mentoring programs in 54, 60, 103–8, 117n36; politics of funding in 19–20; public sector-nonprofit relationships in 98–102, 122

United Way 4–5

Voluntary Action Sheffield (VAS) 120–1

Weiss, Carol 24, 27
Welby, Justin 36
Westminster Interfaith Peace Walk 34
Williams, Rowan 35
World Bank 12
Wythenshawe Strategic Regeneration Framework 78n18

youth *see* children and adolescents
Youth Justice Board 81
Youth Offending Teams 81